Micro-Macramé Jewelry

STYLISH DESIGNS FOR EVERYDAY WEAR

KELSY EASON

Kalmbach Books
21027 Crossroads Circle
Waukesha, Wisconsin 53186
www.JewelryAndBeadingStore.com

Published in 2017
21 20 19 18 17   1 2 3 4 5

Manufactured in China.

ISBN: 978-1-62700-320-9

EISBN: 978-1-62700-321-6

Editor: Dianne Wheeler

Book Design: Lisa Bergman

Technical Editor: Dana Meredith

Proofreader: Annie Pennington

Photographer: William Zuback

Library of Congress Control Number: 2016931495

Micro-Macramé Jewelry

STYLISH DESIGNS FOR EVERYDAY WEAR

KELSY EASON

KALMBACH BOOKS

WAUKESHA, WI

Contents

Introduction

In the beginning … there were knots. From bridge building to horse hitching to sailing and lace making, knots have been an important part of history. Micro-macramé is an updated twist on an old practice.

In an era of instant gratification, there is something empowering about taking a piece of cord or leather and creating a beautiful design from it. However, learning on your own can be difficult, and my desire is to convey the instructions as clearly as possible so that you can pick up the basics, have success from the start, and see satisfying results quickly.

When I first began to explore micro-macramé, I showed my mom a picture of a necklace. She took one look and said, "Oh, so you don't wear it; it's an art piece." Her comment has stuck with me over the years and has inspired me to keep my designs wearable.

When looking at various jewelry designs, I found most items were tightly woven, or highly elaborate and time consuming. My preference is toward more airy designs, so I try to keep my jewelry light. Whether striving for a casual or extravagant piece, I lean toward an open, lacework look.

There are no fancy, expensive tools required for this craft and relatively little space is needed (although it is a good idea to have adequate lighting). Even though some of my patterns use waxed cord or leather, C-Lon cord is my go-to cord. Some bead and craft stores now carry S-Lon cord, which is basically the same thing, just available in fewer colors and the color names are different.

It's time to get creative! Choose your colors, and let's begin. With easy-to-follow, step-by-step instructions, you CAN do this.

It's "knot" hard to learn!

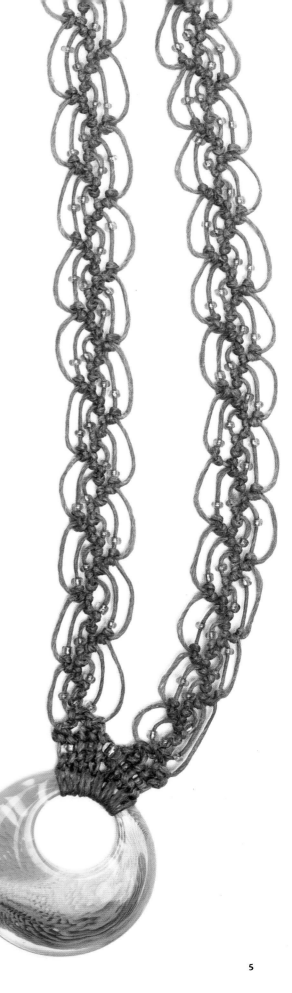

Materials

Types of cording

C-Lon

My patterns often call for a cord called C-Lon cord. It is a 3-ply nylon cord available in a large range of colors. This cord is the standard size for micro-macramé jewelry. It is also available in smaller diameters.

S-Lon

This is the same nylon cord as C-Lon with different color names and a smaller spool-size. It is available in many bead stores and retail hobby and craft stores.

Leather Cord

Available in many colors and sizes, leather cord is available in flat strips and round cord. You can use leather, suede, or faux leather as well. Since leather resists knotting and can break, it is usually only used with less intricate knots, like an overhand knot.

Waxed Linen

As the name implies, this is linen cord lightly coated in wax. It comes in 3-, 4-, or 5-ply and is colorfast. The wax layer prevents fraying, but does add a small amount of bulk to the cord, so tiny diameter beads will not thread onto it.

Types of beads

Metal
Non-precious metals offer a less expensive alternative to silver and gold.

Seed beads
These are often used to embellish my projects, giving them an even more dainty look. They are available in an array of colors, sizes, shapes, and materials.

a

b

Crystal
It is the refraction created by many cuts on a glass surface that gives crystals their fancy shine.

Glass
Lampwork beads (**a**) are designed and made by artists. They offer elegance and sophistication to your piece. Glass beads (**b**) are an excellent choice for novice beaders, as they are more affordable.

Semiprecious or gemstone
These beads are a popular choice as they offer a large variety of options. While the list is extensive, some examples are jade, amber and garnet.

Clay
These beads can be made of stoneware clay, which is fired in a kiln and glazed, or made of porcelain which generally involves a potter's wheel, a kiln, and hand painting. There is also polymer clay which is not technically a clay at all, but a plastic. This material is an oven-baked clay that can be used at home to make your own unique beads and is very versatile.

Other
There are also beads made from shell, such as mother-of-pearl, tiger shell, abalone, and conch shells. You may also come across wooden beads which come from the bark, roots or branches of many types of trees. Some wooden beads are even carved.

Tools

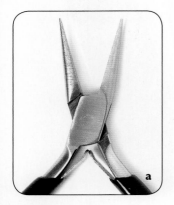

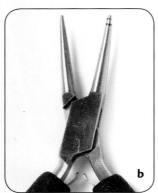

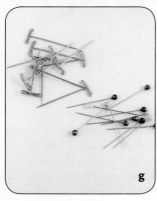

Beading tools

It is a good idea to have some basic beading tools on hand. Several patterns have jump rings or fold-over crimp end closures that will require the use of chainnose **(a)**, roundnose **(b)**, flatnose **(c)**, crimping pliers **(d)**, and/or wire cutters **(e)**. You will also need a pair of small, sharp scissors. If they are not sharp, they will fray the cord.

Reaming tools

It is a lot of fun finding the perfect shape and color of bead, then rushing home to work it into your creation; however, what a disappointment if you then spend hours wrestling with a tiny bead hole which is stubbornly refusing to go onto your cord.

So what is the solution? A simple set of bead reamers **(f)**. I most often use the smallest one, but I've also had occasion to reach for the next size up. Use reamers on glass, ceramic, pearl, and stone beads.

Pins

Straight pins are very important in micro-macramé design work. Some people prefer T-pins. Either way, a long shank is more comfortable to work with. Pins are vital when it comes to holding cords in place and useful for teasing out a mistake without unraveling your cord **(g)**.

Glue

Often in micro-macramé, your only loose ends are at the end of the project when you tie them off. In my experience, this is your weakest link. So why not strengthen it as best as you can? Many people use nail polish; I prefer glue. One type of glue you can use is E6000 **(h)**. It works well on leather, and many jewelry makers prefer to use it over other types of glue.

Personally, I use Beacon 527 multi-purpose glue **(i)**. It dries clear, though shiny. Usually I leave it to dry well (often overnight) then trim my cords and apply a second coat. Some crafters use a singeing tool to fuse the ends of nylon cords, melting them together. This leaves a bit of black residue, so use this technique only on dark cords, or where it won't show (like behind a focal bead or button).

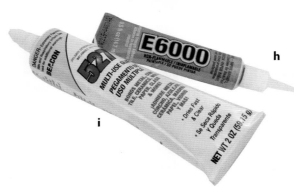

The Essential Project Board

There are several kinds of padded board designs available on the Internet. Some are made of foam and others of cork. When I made mine, I used thick foam to give me the ability to push my straight pin in all the way, using the head to hold the cord tightly when necessary.

1 To make my board, I started with a leftover piece of foam that was lying around. (Ok, it was lying around at my mom's house, but it was in the attic, so it's fair game, right?) I cut it a bit larger than my clipboard. This is about 12" x 13".

note **I have since made a second board and purchased a stiffer type of foam. I like it much better as it has less bounce to it. Then, where the top clip is, I cut out a slope.**

Next, I added about 4" to each side and cut out my fabric. Choose wisely here. On my first try, I used a very light, soft pink, flannel type of fabric. However, I learned quickly, as when I was picking up beads to string onto the cords, I was forever having little bits of fluff on my fingers and in my way. Smooth cotton fabric is a better choice.

2 Cover the foam with fabric. Turn the edges to the back, and safety pin it in place. I like to be able to take the cover off to wash it (there may be a coffee spill in the future) or just change it out if it doesn't work (like the aforementioned pink flannel). Flip the fabric-covered foam over, and fit it onto your clipboard.

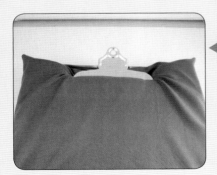

3 I keep straight pins in the top corners of my board. I use them to pin cords, hold fasteners/closures, or to hold a focal bead for a later project.

Basic Knots

Lark's Head Knot

The lark's head knot is most often used when attaching cords to components like jump rings, key rings, or donut beads.

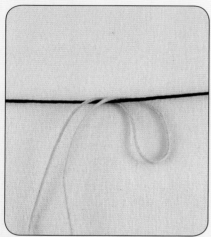  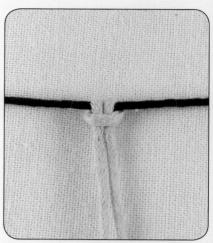

1. Fold a cord in half. Take the center and fold it over a component or cord from front to back.

2. Take the loose end cords and feed them through the loop.

3. Now pull gently and evenly on the ends of the cord to tighten it.

Overhand Knot

This knot is often used at the end of loose cords to keep them from fraying. It is sometimes used at the beginning of a pattern when attaching a cord to other cords.

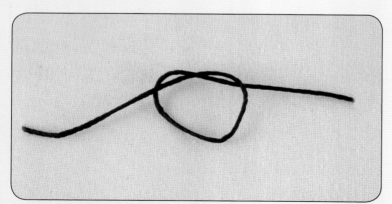

1. Make a loop, push one end through the loop, and pull the cord ends to tighten the knot.

Square Knot (or Flat Knot)

This is one of the most popular knots in micro-macramé. You can work the knot beginning with either the right cord or the left. I usually begin with the left cord. It is most often worked using two outer cords and two or more inner (or filler) cords.

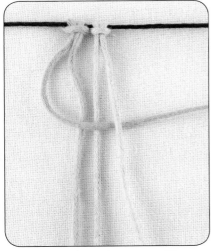

1. Place the left cord over your filler cords. Then place the right cord over the top of the tail of the left cord.

2. Take the right cord and move it under your filler cords, then out and over the left cord.

3. Gently pull the left and right cords to tighten up the first half of the square knot. Now place the right cord over the filler cords. Move the left cord over the top of the tail of the right cord.

4. Place the left cord underneath the filler cords, then out and over the right cord.

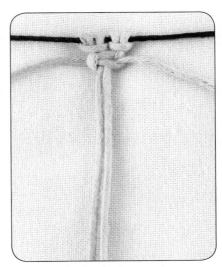

5. Here is the finished square knot.

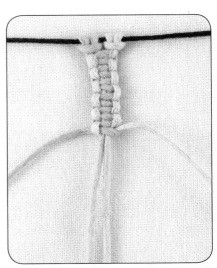

6. Here are several square knots in a row, which is called a *sennit*.

Spiral Knot (or Half Knot)

A half knot is the first half of a square knot. If you tie several in a row, they naturally begin to twist and you get a spiral effect. You can create a left or a right spiral.

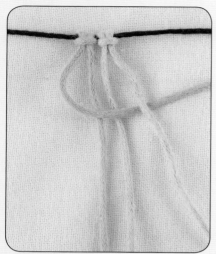

1. To create a left spiral, place the left cord over the filler cords, then put the right cord over the top of the of the left cord.

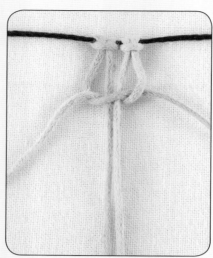

2. Slide the right cord under the filler cords, then out and over the left cord.

3. Tighten it up. Then take the left cord again and put it over the filler cords, moving the right cord over the top of the tail of the left cord.

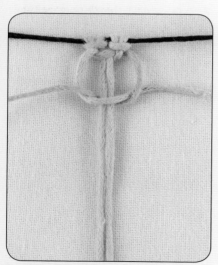

4. Slide the right cord under the filler cords, then out and over the left cord.

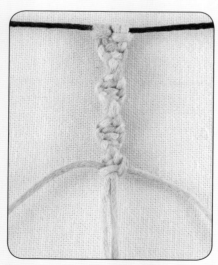

5. Repeat this a few more times and you will see the spiral beginning to form.

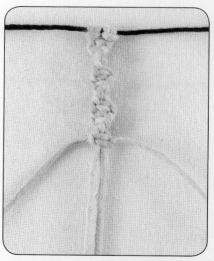

6. To create a right spiral, tie knots from only the right side. Then your spiral will twist the opposite way and look like this.

Diagonal Double Half-Hitch Knot

This knot is a little tricky, but with just a bit of practice you will be able to get a feel for the right amount of tension you need to help you master it. You can work this knot from either side. We will start on the left.

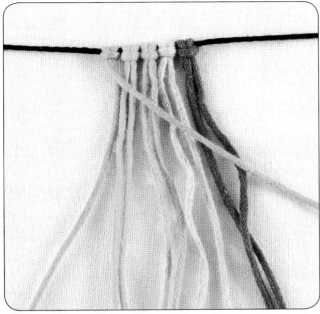

1. Take the far left cord and lay it diagonally over the top of all the other cords. You might want to pin it in place. This is your holding cord, onto which the knots will be tied.

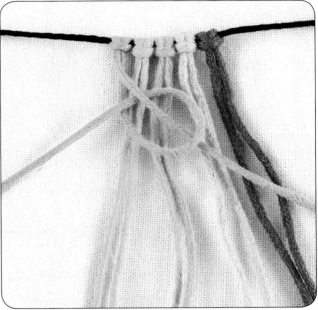

2. Take the cord on the left and, from underneath, wrap it over and around the holding cord. Be sure the tail end of the wrapping cord passes over the cord shaft. Gently snug the knot up to the top of the holding cord.

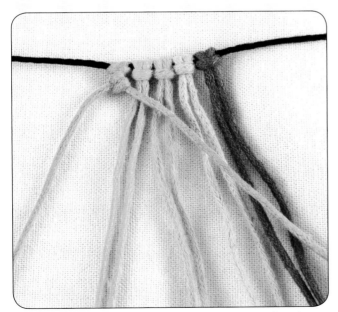

3. Repeat a second time with the same cord to complete the diagonal double half-hitch knot.

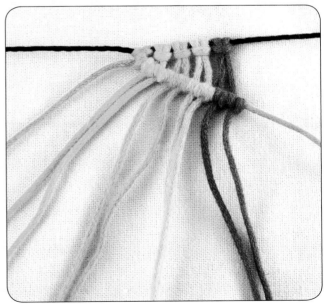

4. Repeat steps 2-3 with the reminaing cords. This is a completed diagonal double half-hitch knot from left to right.

Now we will work a diagonal double half-hitch knot from right to left. I will continue on with the arrangement I have going. Instructions will be the same if you are starting a new project.

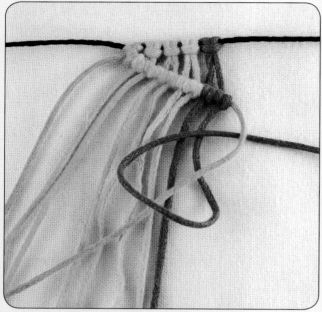

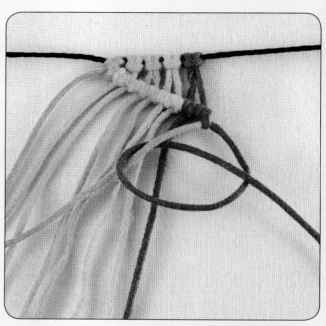

5. Take the cord from the right and lay it diagonally over all the other cords to the left. Pin in place. This is now your holding cord. Working with the adjacent cord, wrap it up around the holding cord, making sure the tail end crosses over its shaft.

6. Snug it up and repeat a second time to finish the knot.

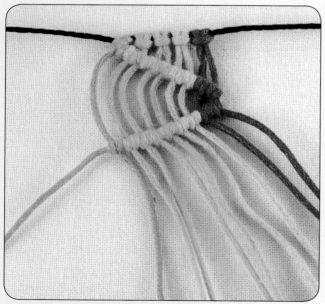

7. Repeat with the remaining cords. This is the completed piece: a row of diagonal double half-hitch knots from left to right, and then from right to left.

Horizontal Double Half-Hitch Knot

This is very similar to the diagonal double half-hitch knot, except for the placement of the holding cord.

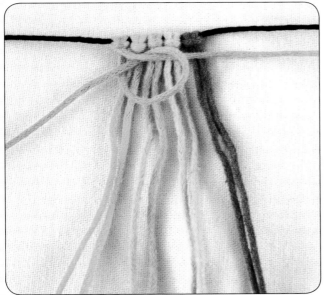

1. Move the left cord to the right, horizontally across the other cords, and pin it in place. Bring the left cord up from below and wrap it over and around the holding cord. Be sure the tail of the wrapping cord passes over the cord shaft.

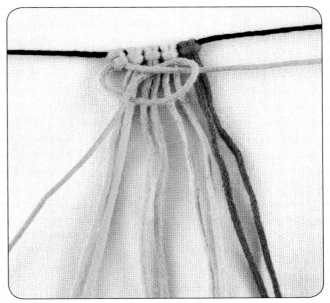

2. Gently snug the knot up to the top of the holding cord. Tighten the knot. Repeat with the same cord to complete a second knot.

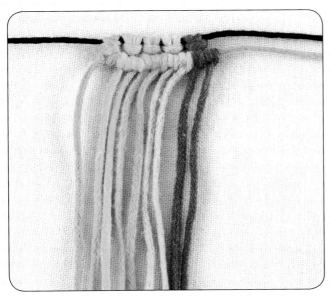

3. Repeat with each cord, keeping the knots tight to the top to create a straight row.

Alternating Lark's Head Chain
(with Vertical Lark's Head Knot variation)

This knot looks harder to make than it really is. Once you get going, it is pretty easy and fun. Just think: over-under-over, then under-over-under.

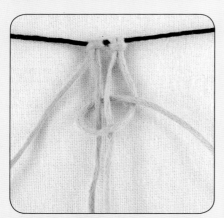

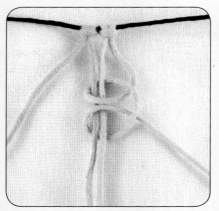

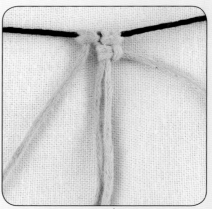

1. Move the right cord and lay it over the center two filler cords, then under the center two cords back to the right, making sure to pass over the shaft of the right cord.

2. You will want to tighten that to the top, but for now I will show you the next half of the knot. Take the right cord and move it under the filler cords then over the center two back to the right, making sure to pass under the shaft of the right cord.

3. Here is what it looks like tightened up.

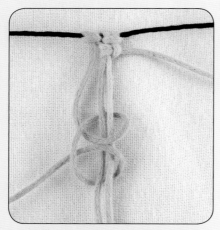

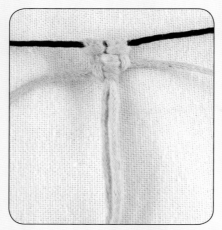

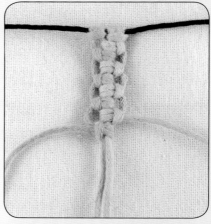

4. Repeat steps 1 and 2 with the left cord (still around the filler cords). Work over, under, over and draw it up tight; then work under, over, under.

5. Here is the second knot tightened up.

6. Alternate sides to create a chain of knots.

Variation

If you tie knots from only one side, it is a Vertical Lark's Head Knot and looks like this.

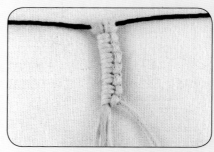

Basic Jewelry Techniques

Plain Loop

1 Trim the wire 3/8 in. (1 cm) above the bead. Make a right-angle bend close to the bead.

2 Grab the wire's tip with roundnose pliers. Roll the wire to form a half circle.

3 Reposition the pliers in the loop and continue rolling, forming a centered circle above the bead.

4 This is the finished loop.

Opening and Closing Jump Rings

1 Hold the jump ring or loop with two pairs of chainnose pliers.

2 To open the jump ring or loop, bring one pair of pliers toward you.

3 Reverse step 2 to close the jump ring or loop.

Folded Crimp

1 Position the crimp bead in the notch closest to the crimping pliers' handle.

2 Separate the wires and firmly squeeze the crimp bead.

3 Rotate the crimp 90-degrees. Move the crimp bead into the notch at the pliers' tip. Squeeze the pliers, folding the bead in half at the indentation.

4 This is the folded crimp.

Fold-Over Crimp End

1 Glue one end of the cord and place it in a fold-over crimp end. Use chainnose pliers to fold one side of the crimp end over the cord.

2 Fold the second side over the first and squeeze gently.

Bracelets

The Red Dragon

Create a flower design with a button closure bracelet using just C-Lon cord, a button, and three beads of various sizes. It works up quickly and has a fun, yet sleek look. The finished length is about 7".

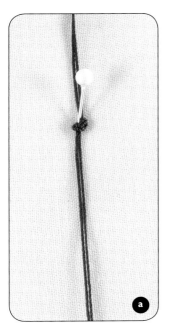

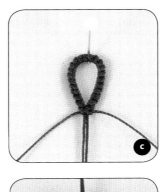

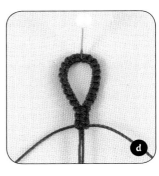

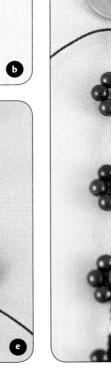

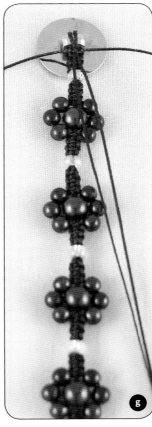

Supplies
- Black C-Lon cord:
  2 cords, 7' each
- **7** 6º clear seed beads
  with silver core
- **36** 4mm burgundy
  beads
- **6** 5mm burgundy
  beads
- **2cm** button
  with shank
- Glue

Instructions

1. Place both cords together, then find the center and tie a loose overhand knot (**Basics, p. 10**). Pin the cords onto your work surface as shown (**a**).

2. Use the right cord to tie about 21 vertical lark's head knots (**Basics, p. 16**) below the overhand knot, then undo the overhand knot (**b**).

3. Bend into a horseshoe shape placing all four cords together. Tie a square knot (**Basics, p. 11**) with the outer two cords. Test the size by placing the button through the button hole. It should fit snugly. Adjust knots as necessary (**c**).

4. Place all cords together and tie two square knots with the outer two cords (**d**).

5. Thread a 6º silver bead onto all four cords. Now tie three square knots.

6. Thread a 5mm burgundy bead onto the center two cords. Thread three 4mm burgundy beads onto each outer cord. Place all four cords together and tie three square knots (**e**).

7. Repeat steps 5 and 6 for desired length, ending with three square knots. (I worked six beaded flowers followed by one silver bead and three square knots to equal about 7".)

8. Thread the button onto the center two cords. Turn to the back side of the bracelet. Now rotate the piece so the button is at the top of your board (**f**).

9. Bring the center two cords back over the button shank, laying them on top of the bracelet. Use the outer cord on each side to tie a square knot around the center cords (but not around the bracelet). Place a dab of glue on the last knot and let it dry. Trim the excess cords (**g**).

Sweet Pea Serenade

In this design, four C-Lon cords need to pass through each of the large beads, so be sure to check the diameter of the hole when purchasing the beads. 6º beads fit several cords through well, while 10º seed beads provide accent color. A classy button completes the look and allows for an easy closure. Finished length is about 7".

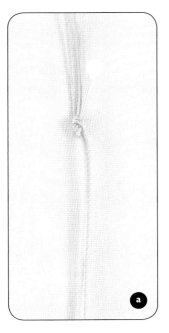

a

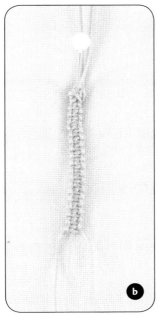

b

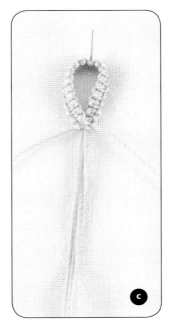

c

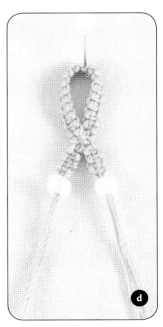

d

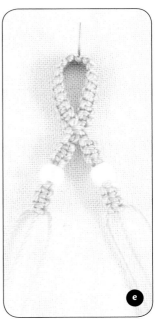

e

Supplies
- Pink C-Lon:
  3 cords, 6' each
- **12** 6º pearlized white seed beads
- **80** 10º gold seed beads
- **5** 1cm pink floral beads
- 1.5cm button with shank
- Glue

Instructions

1. To begin, place three cords together, then find the center and tie a loose overhand knot **(Basics, p. 10)**. Pin onto your work surface as shown **(a)**.

2. Use the outer cords to tie about 18 square knots **(Basics, p. 11)** below the overhand knot, then undo the overhand knot **(b)**.

3. Bend into a horseshoe shape placing all cords together. Tie a square knot with the outer two cords. Test the size by placing the button through the button hole. It should fit snugly. Adjust knots as necessary **(c)**.

4. Separate cords 3-3. With the left three cords, tie three square knots. Thread a 6º white bead onto all three cords. Repeat with the right three cords **(d)**.

5. Tie three square knots with each set of cords **(e)**.

The square knot can be used in several ways; very often to secure a closure. It can be used alone, or you can tie several in a row, which is called a sennit.

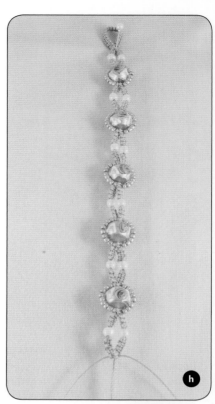

6. Place all cords together and tie a square knot around the four center cords **(f)**.

7. Thread eight 10º gold beads onto each outer cord. Thread a 1cm pink floral bead onto the four center cords. Tie a square knot around the four center cords. **(g)**.

8. Repeat steps 4–7 until you have five 1cm pink floral beads (or more if you want to lengthen it). When you reach your desired size, repeat steps 4–6 **(h)**.

9. Thread the button onto the four center cords. Turn to the back side of the bracelet. Now rotate the piece so the button is at the top of your board **(i)**.

10. Bring the four center cords back over the button shank, laying them on top of the bracelet. Use the outer cord on each side to tie a square knot around the center cords (but not around the bracelet). Add a dab of glue on the last knot and let it dry. Trim the excess cords **(j)**.

Shadow Lands

Working with leather is both fun and challenging. It gives a very different look from other cords, but it can break if you pull too hard. Using a decorative button for the centerpiece gives you a larger hole to work with when placing four leather cords through it. This bracelet is worked from the center out, and the adjustable closure instructions can work with other materials too. Since this type of closure gives a range of size options, I estimate this design gives you a 6"to 8" finished size.

Supplies

- 1mm round, black leather cord:
    - **1** cord, 12"
    - **4** cords, 24" each
- **16** 6º light blue seed beads
- **24** 6º silver seed beads
- 2cm decorative button
- Glue

a

b

c

d

The sliding knot is a popular closure. Square knots are tied around the extra length of cords used to create the piece, allowing the cords to slide freely through the square knots. This convenient closure allows the bracelet to slip over your hand without opening completely.

Instructions

1. Thread two 24" cords through the button and center it, moving the cords down toward the bottom of your work surface **(a)**.

2. Tie a square knot **(Basics, p. 11)** with the outer left and right cords around the inner two cords **(b)**.

3. Thread a 6º silver seed bead onto each outer cord. Using the inner left cord, tie it onto the outer left cord using a vertical lark's head knot **(Basics, p. 16)**. Take the inner right cord and tie it onto the outer right cord using a vertical lark's head knot **(c)**.

4. Thread a 6º silver bead onto each outer cord, then tie a square knot with the outer cords around the inner cords. Tighten cords until snug, but not too tight **(d)**.

5. Thread a 6º light blue bead onto each outer cord. Take the inner left cord and tie it onto the outer left cord using a vertical lark's head knot. Using the inner right cord, tie it onto the outer right cord using a vertical lark's head knot.

6. Thread a 6º light blue bead onto each outer cord, then tie a square knot with the outer cords around the inner cords **(e)**.

7. Repeat steps 3–6 until you reach about 3", then repeat the entire pattern on the other side of the button to create the opposite side of the bracelet.

Adjustable Closure
8. Position end cords so they overlap evenly as shown **(f)**.

9. Position the 12" length of leather horizontally underneath the loose cords **(g)**.

10. Tie four square knots around the end cords to create a slider knot **(h)**.

tip: You want these knots tight, but if you pull too hard, the leather will snap.

11. Trim and glue the ends of this 12" leather cord, taking care not to glue the inside cords. Gently slide the cords through the slider knot to the largest opening you need. Group the cords in pairs and tie an overhand knot **(Basics, p. 10)**, near the slider knot. Trim the end cords **(i)**.

Moonlit Waters

I love that this bracelet is a neutral tone, as it complements many outfits. The rhinestones were a little challenging to find, but I purchased a "finished" bracelet from a craft and bead store, then broke it apart to create something new. Working with C-Lon cord, this sleek, yet elegant bracelet is worked from the center out and is 7" in length, with a graceful toggle clasp closure.

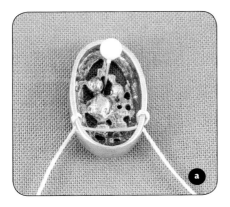 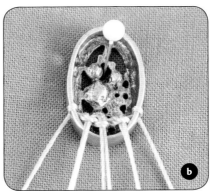 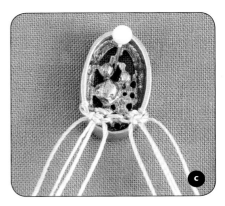

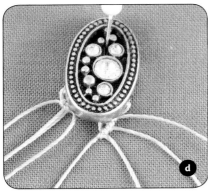 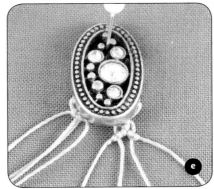 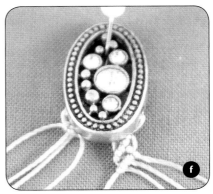

Supplies

- Silver C-Lon cord:
  8 cords, 3½' each
- **12** 6º chrome seed beads
- **8** 5mm rhinestone beads
- **8** 6mm smoky gray beads
- 2cm x 1.5cm centerpiece slider bead
- **2** 5mm silver jump rings
- Toggle clasp
- **2** Pairs of chainnose pliers
- Glue

Instructions

1. Pin the slider bead face down onto your work surface. Center one silver C-Lon cord through the openings on one end. To anchor the cord in place, take the right cord and thread it over and back through the right opening in the silver bead. Take the left cord and thread it over and back through the left opening **(a)**.

2. Take another silver cord, fold it in half, and attach it to the first cord using a lark's head knot **(Basics, p. 10)**. Repeat twice **(b)**.

3. Separate cords 4-4. Tie a square knot **(Basics, p. 11)** with each set of cords **(c)**.

4. Turn the slider bead right side up and separate cords 4-4. Set aside the left four cords.

5. Working with the four right cords, move the second cord from the right to the left as the holding cord. Tie a diagonal double half-hitch knot **(Basics, p. 13)** onto it with each of the left two cords **(d)**.

6. Move the second cord from the right to the right as the holding cord, over the top of the right cord. Tie a diagonal double half-hitch knot onto the holding cord with the right cord **(e)**.

7. Repeat step 5 **(f)**.

Slider beads are beads with two sets of holes to string through. They come in a variety of styles and are generally medium to large in size. They are often used as links or connectors. Here we use one as a centerpiece.

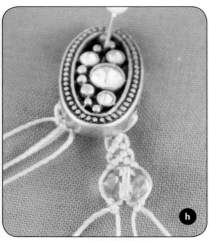

8. Repeat step 6 **(g)**.

9. Thread a 6mm smoky gray bead onto the center two filler cords.

10. Move the left cord to the right and tie a diagonal double half-hitch knot onto it with the second cord from the left.

11. Move the right cord to the left and tie a diagonal double half-hitch knot onto it with the second cord from the right **(h)**.

12. Move the right center cord over the left center cord. Tie a diagonal double half-hitch knot with the center left cord onto the center right cord **(i)**.

13. Move the left cord to the right and tie a diagonal double half-hitch knot onto it with the second cord from the left. Move the right cord to the left and tie a diagonal double half-hitch knot onto it with the second and third cords from the right **(j)**.

14. Thread all four cords through a 6º chrome seed bead.

15. Repeat steps 5 and 6, twice **(k)**.

16. Thread a 5mm rhinestone onto the center two cords.

tip: If you have trouble threading the rhinestone bead, coat the end of the cord with clear nail polish and let dry until it stiffens (for up to an hour or so).

17. Repeat steps 10–15 **(l)**.

18. Repeat steps 9–16.

19. Repeat steps 10–13. Set aside this section.

20. Repeat steps 5–19 using the four left cords **(m)**.

21. Using two pairs of chain-nose pliers, open a jump ring **(Basics, p. 17)**. Attach the silver jump ring to one end of the toggle clasp. Close the jump ring. Turn to the back side of the bracelet and rotate

it so the toggle end is at the top of your board. Thread the center two cords through the jump ring. Bring the center two cords back toward you, laying them on top of the bracelet. Use the outer cord on each side to tie a square knot around the center cords (but not around the bracelet). Place a dab of glue on the last knot and let it dry. Trim the excess cords **(n)**.

22. Repeat with the remaining four cords. Glue and trim ends **(o)**.

23. Repeat steps 1–22 to create the opposite side of the bracelet, using the remaining half of the toggle clasp.

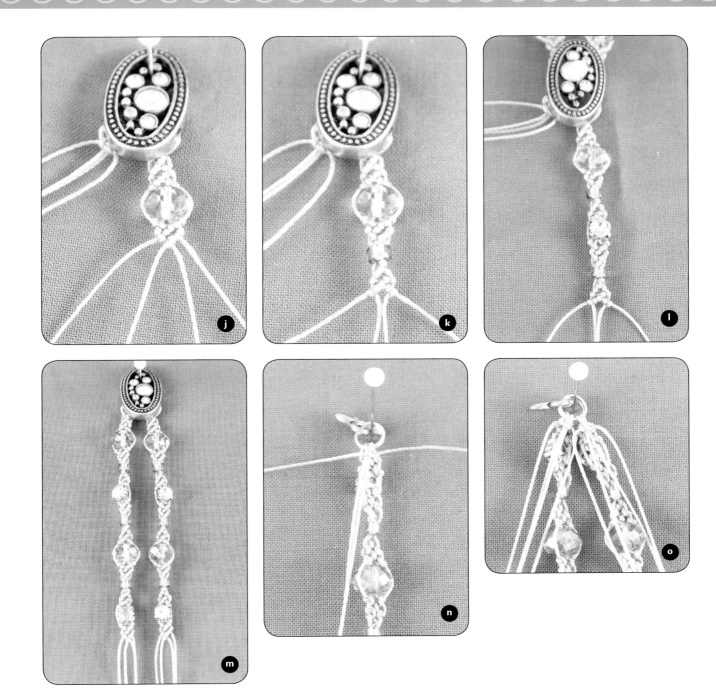

Eternally Yours

This casual wrap pattern offers the look of four different designs in one bracelet. Created using C-Lon cord, it is one long piece with a finished length of about 28" that wraps around the average wrist about four times.

Supplies
- Azalea C-Lon cord: **2** cords, 14½' each
- **21** 6⁰ peacock mix seed beads (dark blue, purple, teal, green)
- **79** 2mm peacock mix beads (dark blue, purple, teal, green)
- **31** 4mm rectangle Rainbow hematite beads
- 7mm button bead
- Glue

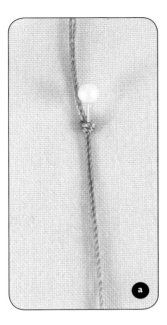

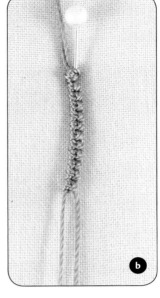

Instructions

1. Place both cords together, then find the center and tie a loose overhand knot (**Basics, p. 10**). Pin it onto your work surface as shown **(a)**.

tip: With long cords like these, I suggest you use a door or cabinet knob to hold the cords while you line up the ends, then follow the cords back to the knob to find the center.

2. Use the right cord to tie about 11 vertical lark's head knots (**Basics, p. 16**) below the overhand knot, then undo the overhand knot **(b)**.

3. Bend into a horseshoe shape placing all four cords together. Tie a square knot (**Basics, p. 11**) with the outer cords. Test your size by placing the button bead through the button hole. It should fit snugly. Adjust knots as necessary **(c)**.

4. Thread a 4mm rectangle Rainbow hematite bead onto the left cord which now becomes the holding cord. Tie a vertical lark's head knot with the second cord from the left onto the left cord (the holding cord), then position the tying cord alongside the holding cord. Using the third cord in from the left and tie a vertical lark's head knot around both holding cords then place this cord with both holding cords. Tie a vertical lark's head knot with the right cord around all three holding cords **(d)**.

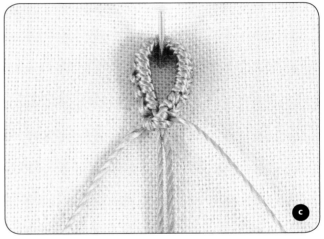

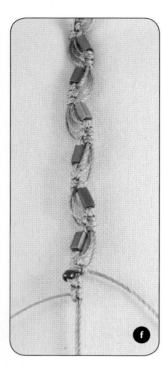

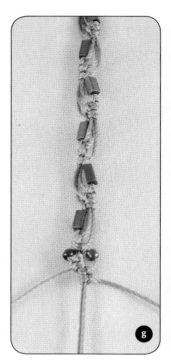

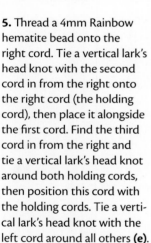

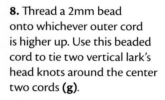
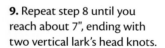

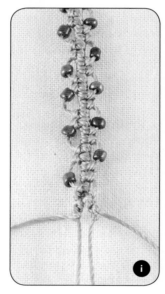
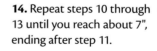

5. Thread a 4mm Rainbow hematite bead onto the right cord. Tie a vertical lark's head knot with the second cord in from the right onto the right cord (the holding cord), then place it alongside the first cord. Find the third cord in from the right and tie a vertical lark's head knot around both holding cords, then position this cord with the holding cords. Tie a vertical lark's head knot with the left cord around all others **(e)**.

6. Repeat steps 4 and 5 until you reach approximately 7" (including the button loop).

7. Set aside the cord that tied the last knot, then thread a 2mm bead (random color order) onto the outer cord on the opposite side. Use this beaded cord to tie two vertical lark's head knots around the center two cords **(f)**.

8. Thread a 2mm bead onto whichever outer cord is higher up. Use this beaded cord to tie two vertical lark's head knots around the center two cords **(g)**.

9. Repeat step 8 until you reach about 7", ending with two vertical lark's head knots.

10. Separate cords 2-2. Move the outer left cord down and right toward the center. Tie a diagonal double half-hitch knot **(Basics, p. 13)** with the second cord in on the left.

11. Move the outer right cord down and left to the center. Tie a diagonal double half-hitch knot with the second cord on the right **(h)**.

12. Repeat steps 10 and 11 **(i)**.

13. Thread a 6º seed bead (random color order) onto all four cords **(j)**.

14. Repeat steps 10 through 13 until you reach about 7", ending after step 11.

15. Find the two longest cords and move one to the outer left and one to the outer right. Tie two square knots.

16. Separate cords 1-3. With the single left cord, thread a 2mm bead, a 4mm bead, and a 2mm bead **(k)**.

17. With the right three cords, tie a right spiral knot **(Basics, p. 12)** for a length of about 1cm, measured from below the vertical lark's head knot.

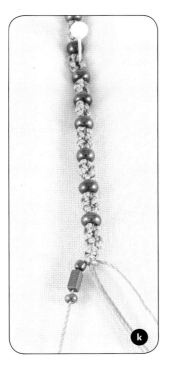

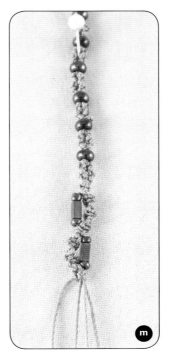

Hematite beads should not be confused with the Rainbow hematite beads used in this project. Most hematite beads are of manmade materials which means they will be a shiny metallic or dark chrome color. However, Rainbow hematite beads have a rainbow hue due to a titanium treatment to the iron ore. Such a beautiful effect!

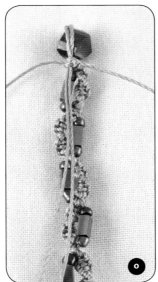

20. With the left cord, tie a vertical lark's head knot around all other cords. The spiral should bow out slightly **(m)**.

21. Repeat steps 16–21 until you reach a length of about 7".

22. Thread the button bead onto the center two cords. Turn the bracelet to the back side and rotate it so the button bead is at the top of your board **(n)**.

23. Bring the two center cords back toward you, laying them on top of the bracelet. Use the outer cord on each side to tie a square knot around the center cords (but not around the bracelet). Place a dab of glue on the last knot and let it dry. Trim the excess cords **(o)**.

18. Use the right cord to tie a vertical lark's head knot around all other cords. The spiral should bow out slightly **(l)**.

19. Separate cords 3-1. Bead the right cord the same as you did the left. With the left three cords, tie a left spiral knot for a length of about 1cm. (Whenver possible, move the shortest cord into the center of the three cords).

Wandering in the Woods

Mainly employing a spiral knot, this bracelet is a versatile piece, easily worked up in any number of color combinations. Choose your charm first, then find colors that complement it. Have fun getting creative with your button closure options. Finished length is about 7".

Supplies
- Fern C-Lon cord:
  2 cords, 9' each
- **4** 6° brown seed beads
- **18** 6° light bronze seed beads
- **5** 7mm cream pearl beads
- **5** 7mm light bronze pearl beads
- **6** 7mm bronze pearl beads
- Charm
- 12" ⅝"-wide sheer brown ribbon
- 6mm jump ring
- 1.5cm button
- **2** Pairs of chainnose pliers (optional)
- Glue

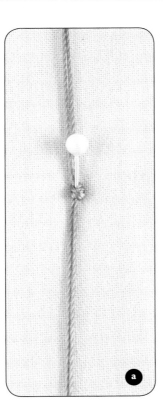

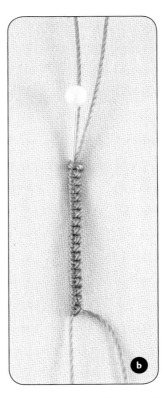

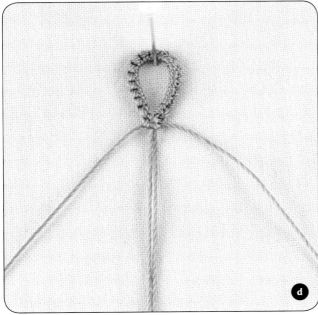

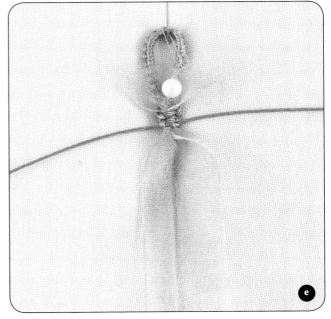

Instructions

1. Place the two cords together and find the center. Tie a loose overhand knot **(Basics, p. 10)** and pin to the board as shown **(a)**.

2. Using the right cord, tie about 19 vertical lark's head knots **(Basics, p. 16) (b)**.

3. Untie the overhand knot and pin to your work surface as shown **(c)**.

4. Place the center two cords together and tie a square knot **(Basics, p. 11)** with the outer two cords. Check to be sure your button fits through snugly. Adjust knots if necessary **(d)**.

5. Lay the ribbon on top of the bracelet and pin in place over the square knot. Don't worry about the excess as it will be trimmed off later. Tie two square knots around the ribbon and the center two cords. Set aside the left cord and the ribbon **(e)**.

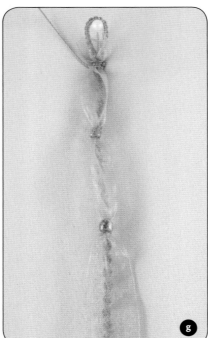

This design takes a little maneuvering when it comes to the braiding aspect. Spend some time getting each part just where you want it to be

6. With the three right cords, use the left cord to tie a left spiral knot (**Basics, p. 12**) for a length of 7" (**f**).

7. Cut the loose end of the ribbon on a diagonal, then roll the edge to help thread on a 6º brown seed bead, positioning it about 1" from the top. Thread another 6º brown bead about 1" below that, and then set the ribbon aside (**g**).

tip: All ribbon beads can be adjusted later to fit the design.

8. On the left cord that was set aside, string beads in the following order: a 6º light bronze pearl, a 7mm bronze seed bead, a 6º light bronze pearl , a 7mm cream pearl, a 6º light bronze pearl, and a 7mm light gold bead. Repeat this beading sequence once.

9. Now thread a 6º light bronze bead, a 7mm bronze pearl, a 6º light bronze bead, a 7mm cream pearl, and a 6º light bronze bead (**h**).

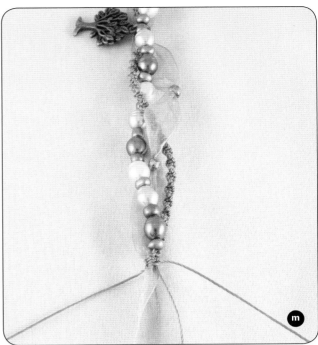

10. Using two pairs of chain-nose pliers, add a jump ring to your charm if needed (**Basics, p. 17**) **(i)**.

11. Beginning with the left beaded cord, loosely braid the three sections together to the end of the beaded section. Thread the ribbon through the jump ring on the charm; thread the spiral knotted cord through; then, thread the beaded cord through it **(j)**.

12. Making sure the beads are snug to the top, thread another 6º light bronze bead on the beaded cord. Pick up the beading sequence where you left off and continue until you have eight 7mm beads on this side of the charm, ending with a 6º light bronze bead **(k)**.

13. Thread two 6º brown seed beads onto the ribbon, spaced about an inch from the charm and about an inch apart **(l)**.

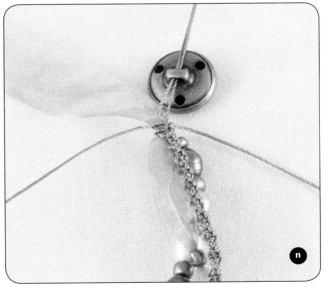

14. Continue braiding loosely, ending with the ribbon on top of all cords. Using the outer cords from the spiral knot, tie two square knots around all cords, including the ribbon. Adjust the placement of the three braided strands as you make the first knot. **(m)**.

15. Thread the button onto the two center cords. Turn to the back side of the bracelet. Now rotate it so the button is at the top of your board **(n)**.

16. Bring the two center cords back over the button shank, laying them on top of the bracelet. Use the outer cord on each side to tie a square knot around the center cords (but not around the bracelet). Tie a second square knot **(o)**.

17. Add a dab of glue to the final knot. Then, using caution (it's easy to catch the wrong cord when trimming the ribbon at the end), cut the excess ribbon and cords on both ends.

Golden Sands

This wave-style bracelet is my take on a classic design. It's a good way to practice the diagonal double half-hitch knot, a great way to use up seed beads, and adapts well to a wide range of color styles. Using a different shape bead at the base of each wave (like the bicone seen here) adds dimension and interest to the design. Finished length is about 7".

Supplies
- Ginger C-Lon cord:
  3 cords, 6' each
- **52** 6° gold seed beads
- **42** 10° light green seed beads
- **49** 10° peach seed beads
- **70** 10° rose seed beads
- **7** 4mm green bicone beads
- 16mm button
- Glue

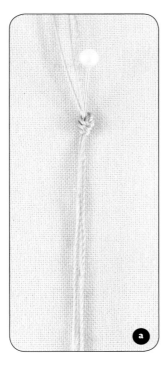

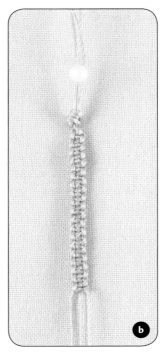

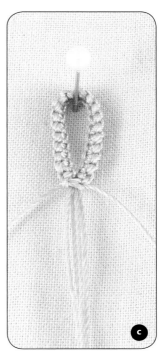

Instructions

1. Place all three cords together, then find the center and tie a loose overhand knot (**Basics, p. 10**). Pin onto your work surface as shown (**a**).

2. Use the outer cords to tie about 19 square knots (**Basics, p. 11**) below the overhand knot, then undo the overhand knot (**b**).

3. Bend into a horseshoe shape placing all six cords together. Tie a square knot with the outer two cords. Test the size by placing the button through the button hole. It should fit snugly. Adjust knots as necessary (**c**).

4. Separate cords 3-3. Tie one square knot with the right three cords, and two square knots with the left three cords (**d**).

5. Move the right cord to the left over all other cords, as the holding cord. Tie a diagonal double half-hitch knot (**Basics, p. 13**) onto the holding cord with each cord from right to left. Repeat (**e**).

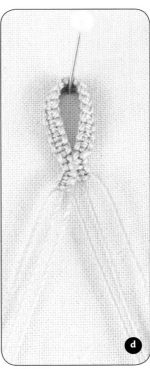

The diagonal double half-hitch knot is actually a half-hitch knot, worked twice. Each half-hitch must be tied onto a cord, usually called the holding cord or the filler cord. It can be tied vertically, horizontally, or diagonally.

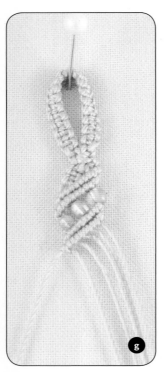

6. Separate cords 2-2-2. Thread each set of cords through a 6º gold seed bead (f).

7. Repeat step 5 (g).

8. Using the left cord, thread beads in the following order: a 10º light green seed bead, a 4mm green bicone bead, and a 10º light green bead.

9. Second cord from the left: thread three 10º peach seed beads.

10. Third cord from the left: thread four 10º rose seed beads.

11. Fourth cord from the left: thread two 10º light green beads, a 6º gold bead, and two 10º light green beads.

12. Fifth cord from left: thread six 10º rose beads.

13. Sixth cord from left: thread a 6º gold bead, two 10º peach beads, a 6º gold bead, two 10º peach beads, and one 6º gold bead (h).

14. Move the left cord to the right over all other cords, as the holding cord. Tie a diagonal double half-hitch knot onto the holding cord with each cord from left to right. Repeat (i).

15. Repeat step 6.

16. Repeat step 14 (j).

17. Using the right cord, thread beads in the following order: a 10º light green bead, a 4mm green bicone bead, and a 10º light green bead.

18. Second cord from the right: thread three 10º peach beads.

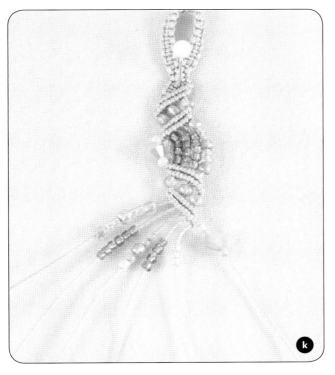

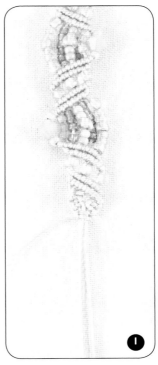

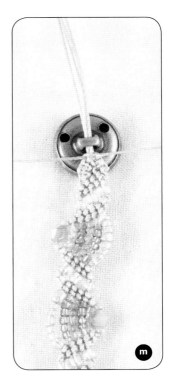

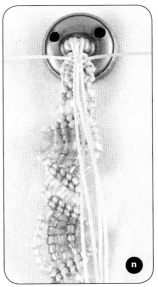

19. Third cord from the right: thread four 10º rose beads.

20. Fourth cord from the right: thread two 10º light green beads, a 6º gold bead, two 10º light green beads.

21. Fifth cord from right: thread six 10º rose beads.

22. Sixth cord from right: thread a 6º gold bead, two 10º peach beads, a 6º gold bead, two 10º peach beads, and a 6º gold bead **(k)**.

23. Repeat steps 5–22 twice. Then repeat steps 5–16 once.

24. Repeat steps 8-23. Then repeat steps 8-16.

tip: This is a 7" bracelet. To lengthen, add another beaded section followed by steps 5,6, and 5. Then skip to step 25 and tie the two square knots on the higher side of the diagonal double half-hitch knot slant.

25. Separate cords 3-3. Tie a square knot with the right three cords, and two square knots with the left three cords. Place all cords together and tie a square knot **(l)**.

26. Thread the button onto the four center cords. Turn to the back side and rotate your piece so the button is at the top of your board **(m)**.

27. Bring the two center cords back over the button shank, laying them on top of the bracelet. Use the outer cord on each side to tie a square knot around the center cords (but not around the bracelet). Place a dab of glue on the last knot and let it dry. Trim the excess cords **(n)**.

Dark Horizon

Adding a bit of height gives us a cuff-style bracelet design. Let's play with waxed linen cord! Waxed linen is a fairly stiff cord, coated with a light wax that holds its shape well. Being thicker than most cords, we are limited to beads with a large diameter hole. We will use primarily 6° seed beads to enhance the black cord. The finished length is about 6½".

Supplies
- Black waxed linen cord:
  12 cords, 30" each
- **6** 6º dark blue seed beads
- **24** 6º light blue seed beads
- **36** 6º silver seed beads
- **48** 2mm silver beads
- **108** 2mm dark blue beads
- 3.5cm focal piece
- 3-to-1 connector
- **2** Silver jump rings
- Lobster claw clasp
- **2** Pairs of chainnose pliers
- Glue

Instructions

1. Fold a cord in half. Attach it to the center of the center piece using a lark's head knot (**Basics, p. 10**) (**a**).

2. Center a second cord horizontally under these two cords, just below the lark's head knot. Tie it onto the center cords using an overhand knot (**Basics, p. 10**) (**b**).

3. Repeat steps 1 and 2 to the right, then again to the left (**c**).

4. With each set of four cords, tie a square knot (**Basics, p. 11**) with the outer left and right cord around the two inner cords.

5. Find the center set of four cords. Thread a 6º silver seed bead, a 6º dark blue bead, and a 6º silver bead onto the two center cords. Onto each outer cord, thread two 2mm silver seed beads, a 6º silver bead, and two 2mm silver beads.

6. On the two center cords of the four left cords, thread a 6º light blue bead, a 6º silver bead, and 6º light blue seed bead. Repeat with the center two cords of the right section (**d**).

7. On the four left cords, thread two 2mm dark blue beads onto the left and right cords. Thread the right cord through the 6º silver bead from the left cord of the center section. Thread two 2mm dark blue beads onto this cord and three onto the left cord.

8. On the four right cords, thread two 2mm dark blue beads onto the left and right cords. Thread the left cord through the 6º silver bead from the right cord of the center section. Thread two 2mm dark blue beads onto this cord and three onto the right cord **(e)**.

9. Separate cords 4-4-4. Tie three square knots with each set of cords **(f)**.

10. Repeat steps 5 through 9 to create three beaded sections followed by three square knots **(g)**.

11. Repeat steps 1–10 to make the opposite side of the bracelet.

12. Turn to the back of the bracelet. With each set of four cords, thread the two center cords under and through one loop of a 3-to-1 connector. Bring the center cords back toward you, laying them on top of the bracelet. Snug the connector up to the bracelet.

13. Bring the left and right cords to the back. Tie a square knot around the two center cords. Repeat on the opposite end of the bracelet. Glue and trim the excess cords. **(h)**

14. Open a jump ring **(Basics, p. 17)**. Attach a jump ring to one end of the connector. Close the jump ring. Attach a jump ring and a lobster claw clasp to the other end **(i)**.

Morning Mist

Even though this is a tri-colored bracelet, it is actually worked in sets of two. The two center cords are knotted with the two cords next to them (first to the left, then to the right). After working with two colors, two beads are added. To create the pattern, each holding cord gets two knots added onto it. Finished length is about 6½".

Supplies

- Steel C-Lon cord:
  2 cords, 36" each
- Blue morning C-Lon cord:
  2 cords, 36" each
- Silver C-Lon cord:
  2 cords, 36" each
- **44** 3mm pearl beads
- 3.5cm centerpiece
- 5mm silver jump ring
- Silver toggle clasp
- **2** Pairs chainnose pliers
- Glue

Instructions

1. Fold a steel C-Lon cord in half to find the center and attach it to the centerpiece using a lark's head knot **(Basics, p. 10)**. To the right of this cord, attach a blue morning cord, then a silver C-Lon cord **(a)**.

2. Take the third cord from the left and move it to the left to act as the holding cord. Tie a diagonal double half-hitch knot **(Basics, p. 13)** onto it with each of the next two cords working from inside to outside **(b, c)**.

3. Move the fourth cord from the left and place it to the left as the holding cord. Tie a diagonal double half-hitch knot onto it with each of the next two cords, working from inside to outside **(d, e)**.

4. Move the third cord from the right, moving it to the right as the holding cord. Tie a diagonal double half-hitch knot onto it with each of the next two cords, working from inside to outside **(f, g)**.

5. Move the fourth cord from the right, to the right as the holding cord. Tie a diagonal double half-hitch knot onto it with each of the next two cords, working from inside to outside **(h)**.

6. Thread a 3mm pearl bead onto each outer cord **(i)**.

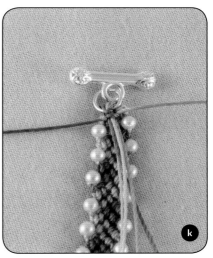

7. Repeat steps 2–5 until you have 11 beads per side (or more if you want to lengthen it) ending after step 6.

8. For one side of the closure: Thread the loop half of a toggle clasp onto the four center cords. Turn to the back side of the bracelet. Now rotate so the clasp is at the top of your board. Bring the four center cords back toward you, laying them on top of the bracelet, snugging up to the toggle clasp. Use the outer cord on each side to tie a square knot around the center cords (but not around the bracelet). Place a dab of glue on the last knot and let it dry. Trim excess cords **(j)**.

9. Repeat steps 1–7 for the opposite side and repeat step 12, threading the four center cords through a jump ring (keeping the opening available). Once you have finished step 12, using two pairs of chainnose pliers, attach the jump ring to the bar of the toggle clasp **(Basics, p. 17) (k)**.

Whispering Bamboo

Whether you're having trouble finding just the right focal piece or you are looking for something completely unique, this fun flower pendant hits the mark. I prefer the look when using 11º seed beads on the petals, but it is not always possible to match the color and size, so here I have used 10º. The choice is yours! This is an over-the-head type of necklace, so be sure to cut the suede cord to your desired length.

Supplies

- Blush C-Lon cord:
    - **1** cord, 4'
    - **1** cord, 5'
- **6** 6º antique gold seed beads
- **28** 10º brown seed beads
- **28** 10º cream seed beads
- **58** 10º copper seed beads
- 5mm round brown bead
- **6** 9mm oval copper beads
- **2** 1cm antique gold connector rings
- 5mm antique gold jump ring
- **2** 2mm (or 2.5mm) gold crimp beads
- 4' of ⅛"-wide chocolate suede cord
- Tapestry needle
- **2** Pairs chainnose pliers
- Crimping pliers
- Glue

Suede cord is available in many widths and colors. If you prefer, you can also use faux-suede cord made from microfibers.

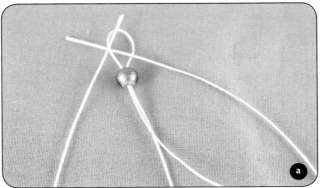

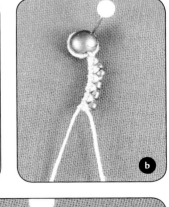

Instructions

Flower Pendant:

1. Fold the 5' C-Lon cord in half and place both ends together. Now, thread the 5mm brown bead onto the cord, sliding it down until you can leave just a slight loop at the other end. Thread one of the loose ends of cord through the loop. Thread the other cord through from the opposite side. Tighten the cords, end **(a)**.

2. Use the right cord to tie a vertical lark's head knot **(Basics, p. 16)** onto the left cord.

3. Thread a 10º seed bead onto the right cord. Tie a vertical lark's head knot with the right cord onto the left cord. Repeat four times **(b)**.

4. Thread a 9mm oval bead onto the left cord, then thread the tapestry needle onto the same cord. Thread the right cord through the oval bead as well. Using the tapestry needle, thread it from the bottom up, to the left of the first seed bead, causing the beaded section to curve up and in, resting the oval bead next to the seed bead section **(c)**.

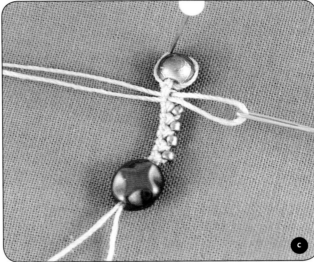

5. With the needle still attached to the cord, move this same cord next to the 5mm brown bead, threading it from the front to the back **(d)**.

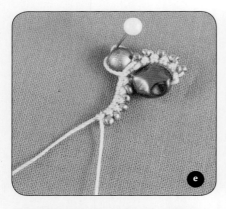

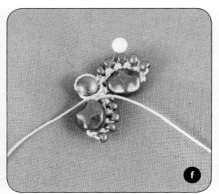

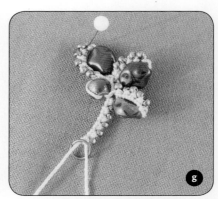

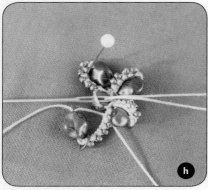

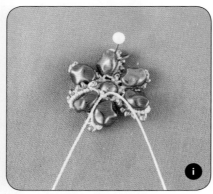

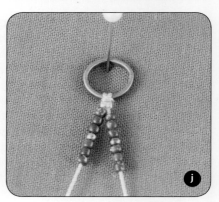

6. Using the cord exiting the oval bead, tie a vertical lark's head knot onto the cord with the tapestry needle on it. Then repeat step 3 **(e)**.

7. Remove the tapestry needle. Keeping the seed beads to the right of the oval bead, repeat steps 4 and 5. (Now the first & second petals are finished.) **(f)**

8. Repeat steps 6 and 7 to complete the third petal. Next, repeat step 6 with two minor changes to the pattern: First, on the fourth petal (just before threading the oval bead), thread a jump ring onto both cords. (The necklace will be attached here later.) **(g)**

Second, use the tapestry needle as before, threading it from the bottom up, to the left of the first seed bead. Now, with the needle still attached to the cord, move the same cord next to the 5mm brown bead, threading it from the top to the bottom on the open side of the bead **(h)**.

9. Repeat step 6.

10. Repeat step 7.

11. Repeat step 6.

12. Remove the tapestry needle and repeat steps 4 and 5.

13. Using the cord exiting the oval bead, tie a vertical lark's head knot onto the cord with the tapestry needle still on it.

14. Turn to the back and tie an overhand knot (**Basics, p. 10**) with both cords. Tie a second overhand knot. Glue this last knot then trim the excess cords **(i)**.

Necklace:
1. Fold the 4' C-Lon cord in half and attach it to a 1cm antique gold connector ring using a lark's head knot (**Basics, p. 10**). Thread a crimp bead onto both cords and close using crimping pliers (**Basics, p. 17**).

2. On the left cord, thread beads in the following order: three 10º brown seed beads, a 10º copper seed bead, and three 10º brown beads. Repeat this pattern on the right cord **(j)**.

3. Thread both cords through a 6º antique gold seed bead.

4. On the left cord, thread beads in the following order: three 10º copper beads, a 10º cream seed bead, and three 10º copper beads. Repeat this pattern on the right cord.

5. Repeat step 3 **(k)**.

6. On the left cord, thread beads in the following order: three 10º cream beads, a 10º brown bead, and three 10º cream beads. Repeat the pattern on the right cord.

7. Repeat step 3 **(l)**.

8. Thread both cords through the jump ring on the flower pendant, then repeat step 3.

9. Repeat steps 6 and 3.

10. Repeat steps 4 and 3.

11. Repeat step 2 **(m)**.

12. Thread both cords through a 2mm crimp bead. Thread both cords from front to back through a 1cm antique gold connector ring, then back through the crimp bead. Close the crimp bead and trim the excess cords.

13. Fold the 4' suede cord in half. Attach it to one of the connector rings using a lark's head knot. Smooth both cords, thread them through the remaining ring, and tie an overhand knot. Glue the knot and trim the excess cords **(n)**.

Simply Timeless

The slightly romantic look of this piece makes it one of my favorites. Have fun choosing a fabulous toggle clasp to accent this switch knot necklace. With a little knotting, some beading and a bit of time, this blush C-Lon cord turns into a simply elegant piece. The finished length is 14".

Supplies
- Blush C-Lon cords: **2** cords, 8' each
- **46** 6$^\text{o}$ antique gold seed beads
- **128** 10$^\text{o}$ dark rose seed beads
- **16** 4mm pink champagne beads
- **32** 4mm light pink bicone beads
- **16** 5mm pink champagne beads
- **2** 2mm gold crimp beads
- 1" toggle clasp
- Crimping pliers

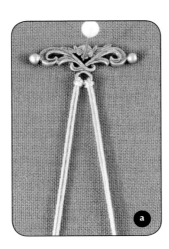

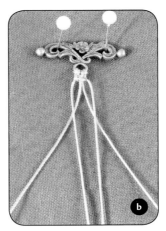

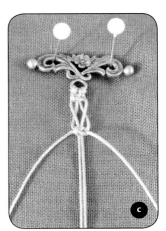

Instructions

1. Fold an 8' cord in half to find the center. Attach this cord to the bar end of a toggle clasp using a lark's head knot (**Basics, p. 10**). Repeat with the second cord **(a)**.

2. Use the outer left and right cord to tie a square knot (**Basics, p. 11**). Move the outer left and outer right cords into the center, over the top of the other cords. Leave a 1cm space and tie a square knot with the outer left and outer right cord. Now you've created a "switch knot" **(b, c)**.

3. Thread four cords through a 6$^\text{o}$ antique gold seed bead and tie a square knot. Thread a 4mm light pink bicone bead onto the two center cords. Then tie a square knot with the outer two cords, leaving the cords a little loose around the bead. Now thread all four cords through another 6$^\text{o}$ antique gold bead. Tie a square knot **(d)**.

A clasp can be both beautiful and functional as we see in this pattern. Toggle clasps are easy to use and are favored due to the decorative nature they bring to a design.

4. Repeat steps 2 and 3 until you have created 17 switch knots, ending after step 2.

5. Thread all four cords through a 2mm gold crimp bead and gently snug it against the last knot. Close the crimp bead tightly **(Basics, p. 17)**. Then carefully trim only the left cord and the right cord, leaving the two center cords for beading **(e)**.

6. Thread beads onto the left cord in the following order: two 10º dark rose seed beads, a 5mm pink champagne bead, two 10º dark rose beads, a 4mm pink bicone bead, two 10º dark rose beads, a 5mm pink champagne bead, two 10º dark rose beads, and a 6º antique gold bead. Repeat this patern until you have 16 5mm pink champagne beads. Thread two 10º dark rose beads after the last 5mm pink champagne bead, omitting the last 6º antique gold bead **(f)**.

7. Repeat step 6 on the right cord, but use a 4mm pink champagne bead instead of a 5mm pink champagne bead. Bead until you have added 16 4mm pink champagne beads. Thread two 10º dark rose beads after the last 4mm pink champagne bead, omitting the last 6º antique gold bead **(g)**.

e

f

g

h

8. Thread both cords through a 2mm crimp bead, the large toggle closure (front to back), then back through the crimp bead. Snug up against the toggle, and close the crimp bead. Trim the excess cords **(h)**.

Endless Sunset

"Messy elegance" at its best! This playful necklace is made using knotted cords mixed with strands of beads and chain. It works up quickly and is a good way to use up extra seed beads while offering flexible color options. This necklace measures 24" in length.

Supplies

- Chocolate C-Lon cords:
  2 cords, 6' each
  2 cords, 2' each
- China Coral C-Lon cords:
  2 cords, 6' each
  2 cords, 2' each
- **11** 6° brown seed beads
- **20** 6° gold seed beads
- **26** 6° coral seed beads
- **126** 2mm brown beads
- **158** 2mm cream beads
- **7** 7mm round coral beads
- **12"** chain, 7-10mm links
- **13"** chain 6-7mm links
- **11** gold jump rings
- **2** 1.5cm gold connector ring
- **4** 1.3mm gold crimp beads
- Gold spring ring clasp
- Crimping pliers
- Glue

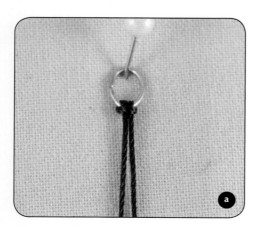

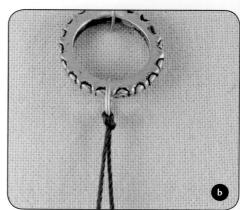

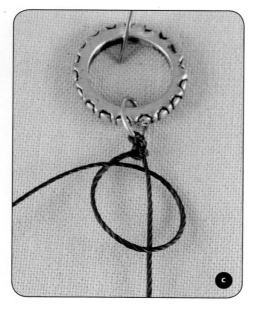

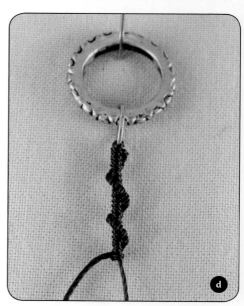

Instructions

1. Fold a 6' chocolate C-Lon cord in half. Attach it to a gold jump ring using a lark's head knot (**Basics, p. 10**) **(a)**.

2. Open a jump ring (**Basics, p. 17**) and attach it to a 1.5cm gold connector ring. Close the jump ring **(b)**.

3. Using the left cord, tie 10 double half-hitch knots onto the right cord **(c, d)**. The double half-hitch knot is tied the same as a diagonal double half-hitch knot, but instead of moving the holding cord to the diagonal, keep the holding cord vertical.

4. Onto both cords, thread beads in the following order: a 6° coral seed bead, a 6° gold seed bead, a 7mm coral bead, a 6° gold bead, and a 6° coral bead **(e)**.

5. Repeat steps 3 and 4, moving the shortest cord to the right when beading, until you reach about 10½"; ending with the knotted section.

6. Thread both cords through a jump ring, then rotate so the jump ring is at the top of your board. Bring the shorter cord back over the top of the knots. Use the longer cord to tie a double half-hitch knot around other cord. Glue the knot, then trim the excess cords **(f)**.

7. Fold a 6' China coral C-Lon cord in half. Attach it to a jump ring using a lark's head knot.

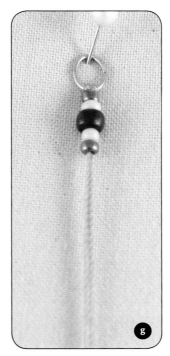

8. Onto both cords, thread beads in the following order: a 2mm gold bead, a 6º cream bead, a 3mm brown bead, then a 6º cream bead, and a 2mm gold bead **(g)**.

9. Using the left cord, tie 10 double half-hitch knots onto the right cord **(h)**. (As in step 3, the double half-hitch knot is tied the same as a diagonal double half-hitch knot, but instead of moving the holding cord to the diagonal, keep the holding cord vertical.)

10. Repeat steps 7 and 8 until you reach about 12¼", ending with a beaded section.

11. Thread both cords through a jump ring, then rotate so the jump ring is at the top of your board. Bring the shorter cord back over the top of the beads. Use the longer cord to tie a double half-hitch knot around the other cord. Glue the knot and then trim the excess cords **(i)**.

12. Thread the 2' chocolate C-Lon cord through a crimp bead, through a jump ring, and then back through the crimp bead. Close the crimp. **(Basics, p. 17)**. Trim the short cord.

13. Thread the cord with 18 2mm brown beads, a 6º coral bead, a 6º gold bead, and a 6º coral bead. Repeat for about 11½" **(j)**.

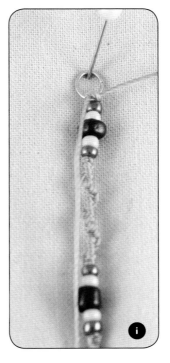

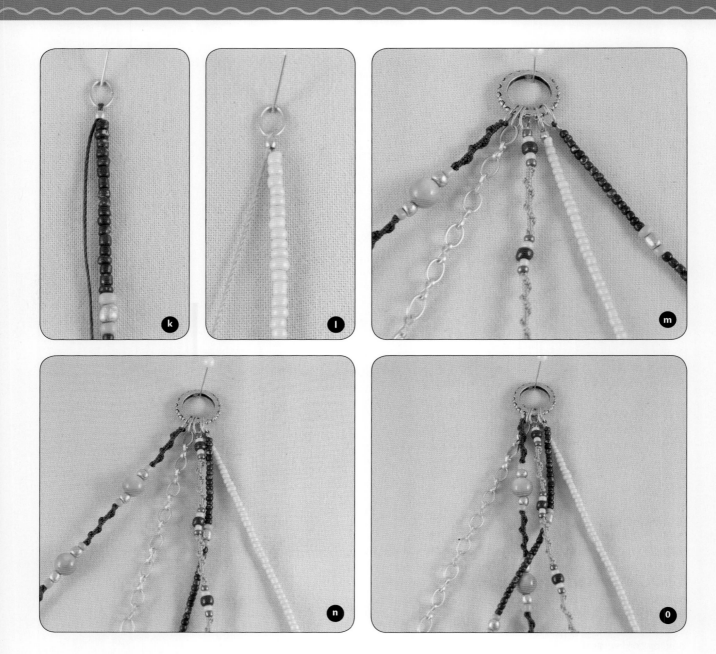

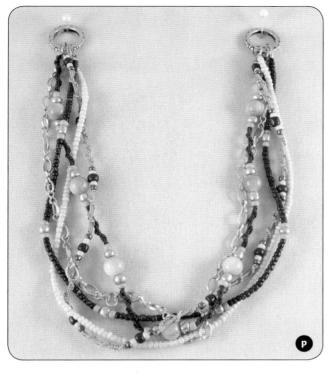

14. Thread the cord through a crimp bead, a jump ring and back through the crimp bead. Close the crimp. Trim the excess cord. **(k)**.

15. Thread the 2' China coral C-Lon through a crimp bead, a jump ring, and back through the crimp bead. Close the crimp. Trim the short cord.

16. Thread the cord with 12" of 2mm cream beads. Then thread the cord through a crimp bead, a jump ring, and back through the crimp bead. Close the crimp. Trim the excess cord. **(l)**.

17. If needed, attach a jump ring to the 13" 6-7mm link chain .

18. Using the chocolate C-Lon cord with the connector ring, attach the remaining strands as shown **(m)**.

19. Braid the five strands loosely together: Think of the strands as numbered 1 through 5, from left to right. Pass cord 5 (the right cord) over 4 and under 3 **(n)**.

20. Pass cord 1 over 2 and under the new 3 cord **(o)**.

21. Repeat steps 19 and 20 until you have loosely braided all strands together.

22. Attach the end jump rings to the second connector ring **(p)**.

23. Cut a 6" length of the 7-10mm chain. Using a jump ring, attach a spring ring closure to one end. On the other end, use a jump ring to attach the chain and one of the connector rings **(q)**.

24. Attach a jump ring to one end of the remaining 7-10mm link chain. On the other end, use a jump ring to attach the chain and the remaining connector ring.

Shimmering Raindrops

This captivating choker is worked with C-Lon cord from the focal bead out. The sides work up quickly, then you create the spiral knot section, and bead a little wire to complete the piece. It has a finished length of about 14" and is designed with an adjustable 3" extender.

Supplies

- Eggplant C-Lon cord:
    4 cords, 36" each
    6 cords, 60" each
- **26** 6º silver seed beads
- **96** 11º chrome seed beads
- 4cm focal piece
- **76** 2mm black beads
- **16** 3mm dark red bicone beads
- **6** 6mm chrome or black beads
- **6** 10mm chrome or black rings
- **3** Flat silver spacer beads
- Silver headpin
- **2** Fold-over crimp ends
- 22-Gauge silver wire:
    5" and 4" pieces (one each)
- Adjustable closure with lobster clasp, 3"
- Wire cutters
- Chainnose pliers
- Roundnose pliers
- Glue

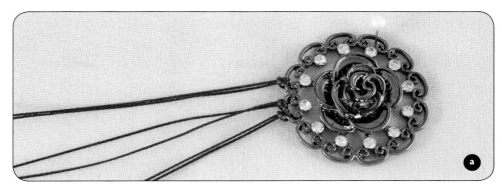

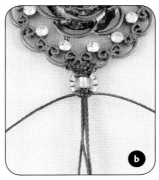

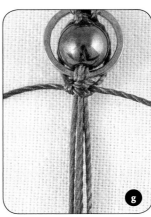

Instructions

1. Fold a 60" cord in half. Attach it to the focal piece using a lark's head knot (**Basics. p. 10**). Attach the first cord; then attach the second and third cords in the section below the first cord (**a**).

2. Turn so the focal bead is at the top of your board with the cords running straight down. Tighten the lark's head knots. Tie a square knot (**Basics, p. 11**) with the left and right cords around the center four filler cords.

3. Thread the center four filler cords though a 6º silver seed bead. Thread three 11º chrome seed beads onto each outer cord. Tie a square knot with the left and right cords around the four center filler cords (**b**).

4. Separate cords 2-2-2. On the second cord from the left, thread a 2mm black bead. Tie a vertical lark's head knot (**Basics, p. 16**) with the left cord onto the cord next to it, leaving a slight curve on the outer cord. Repeat twice more (**c**).

5. On the second cord from the right, thread a 2mm black bead. Tie a vertical lark's head knot with the outer right cord onto the cord next to it, leaving a slight curve on the outer cord. Repeat twice.

6. Thread both center cords through a 3mm dark red bicone bead (**d**). Place all cords together. Tie a square knot with the outer two cords around the four center filler cords.

7. Repeat step 3 (**e**).

8. Thread the center four cords through a 10mm ring. With the outer cords, tie a square knot at the top of the ring. (Both cords tying the square knot will glide over the top of the ring.) (**f**)

9. Place a 6mm black bead onto the center cords. If possible, thread it onto all four cords. If not, thread the center two cords through the bead and move the other two cords underneath the bead, to the back of the ring. Thread the left and right cords down through the ring, then tie a square knot at the bottom of the ring (**g**).

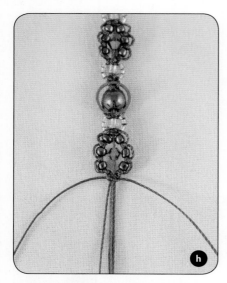

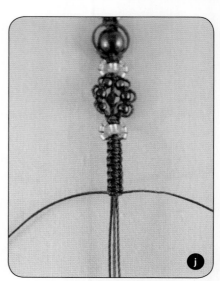

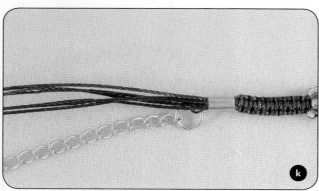

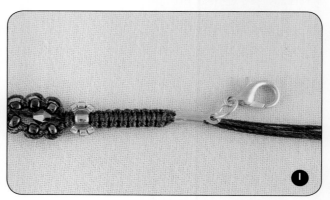

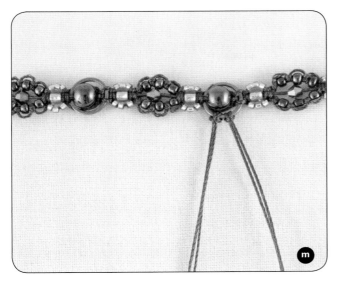

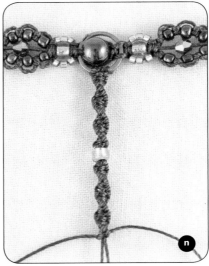

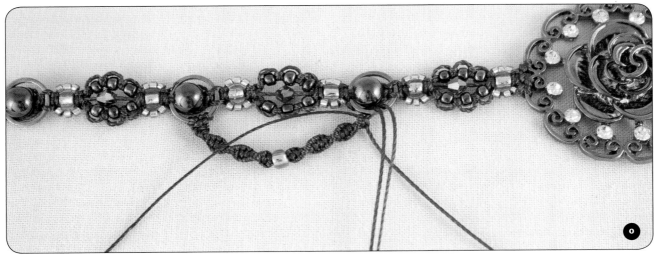

10. Repeat step 3.

11. Repeat steps 4–6 **(h)**.

12. Repeat step 3.

13. Repeat steps 8 and 9 **(i)**.

14. Repeat step 3.

15. Repeat steps 4–6.

16. Repeat step 3.

17. Repeat steps 8 and 9.

18. Repeat step 3.

19. Repeat steps 4–6.

20. Repeat step 3.

21. Place all cords together and tie seven square knots with the outer cords **(j)**.

22. Repeat steps 1–16 to complete the opposite side of the necklace.

23. Check the length and add or subtract square knots as necessary, keeping in mind we are using an adjustable closure. Add a dot of glue to one side of a ribbon clasp. Turn the necklace over so the back side is up. On one end, position the cords in the clasp. Use chainnose pliers to close the fold-over crimp end. **(Basics, p. 17)**. Trim the excess cords **(k)**.

24. Using the second part of the closure, repeat on the other end of the necklace **(l)**.

25. Place the necklace right side up across your work surface. Fold one of the 36" cords in half to find the center. Attach it to the second metal ring from the left using a lark's head knot. Repeat with a second 36" cords **(m)**.

26. Position the four cords together and use the left cord to tie a left spiral knot **(Basics, p. 12)** for a length of about ¾".

27. Thread all four cords through a 6⁰ silver bead. Continue tying spiral knots for another ¾" **(n)**.

28. Move the spiral up and to the right. Thread the center two cords through the third ring from back to front **(o)**.

29. Repeat steps 26 and 27, moving the shortest cords to the center position when beading.

30. Thread the center two cords through an opening on the focal piece from front to back. Turn the necklace over to the back and, using the outer two cords, tie a square knot **(p)**.

31. Glue and trim the cords.

32. Place the necklace right side up across your work surface. Fold one of the 36" cords in half. Attach it to the second metal ring from the right using a lark's head knot. Repeat with a second 36" cord.

33. Use the right cord to tie a right spiral knot for a length of about ¾".

34. Thread all four cords through a 6º silver bead. Continue tying the spiral knot for another ¾".

35. Move the spiral up and to the left. Thread the center two cords through the third ring from the right from back to front.

36. Repeat steps 32 and 33, moving the shortest cords to the center position when beading.

37. Thread the center two cords through an opening on the focal piece from front to back. Turn the necklace over to the back and, using the outer two cords, tie a square knot.

38. Glue and trim the cords. Turn the piece to the front.

Focal Piece Dangle

39. Cut a 4" piece of 22-gauge wire with wire cutters. Use roundnose pliers to make a plain loop **(Basics, p. 17)** on one end of the wire. Attach it to the center left opening of the focal piece where the C-Lon cord is attached.

tip: Make sure the plain loop is big enough to accommodate the edges of the focal piece.

40. String beads in this order: a 6º silver bead, 3 2mm black beads, a dark red bicone bead, 3 2mm black beads, a silver spacer bead, 3 2mm black beads, a dark red bicone, 3 2mm black beads, and a 6º silver bead.

41. Snug the beads to the left and curve the wire up to the right. Use roundnose pliers to make a plain loop near the end of the beads. Attach the loop to the opening on the right of the focal piece where the C-Lon attached **(q)**.

42. On a silver head pin, string a dark red bicone, a silver spacer, a 6mm black bead, a silver spacer, and a dark red bicone. Make a plain loop at the top with round-nose pliers **(r)**.

43. Cut a 5" piece of 22-gauge wire. Use roundnose pliers to make a plain loop on one end. Attach it to the same opening in the focal piece as before, to the left of the first wire.

44. String beads in the following order: a 6° silver bead, 2 2mm black beads, a dark red bicone, 2 2mm black beads, a 6° silver bead, 2 2mm black beads, a dark red bicone, and 2 2mm black beads.

45. Thread the headpin unit onto the wire, and then continue adding beads in the following order: 2 2mm black beads, a dark red bicone, 2 2mm black beads, a 6° silver bead, 2 2mm black beads, a dark red bicone, 2 2mm black beads, a 6° silver bead.

46. Snug the beads to the left and curve the wire up to the right. Use roundnose pliers to make a plain loop near the beads. Attach the loop to the same opening in the focal piece as before, to the right of the first wire **(s)**.

tip: If your focal piece has one opening per side, position all three cords together in the same place. This picture shows a slight variation of this pattern, because of the focal piece's structure.

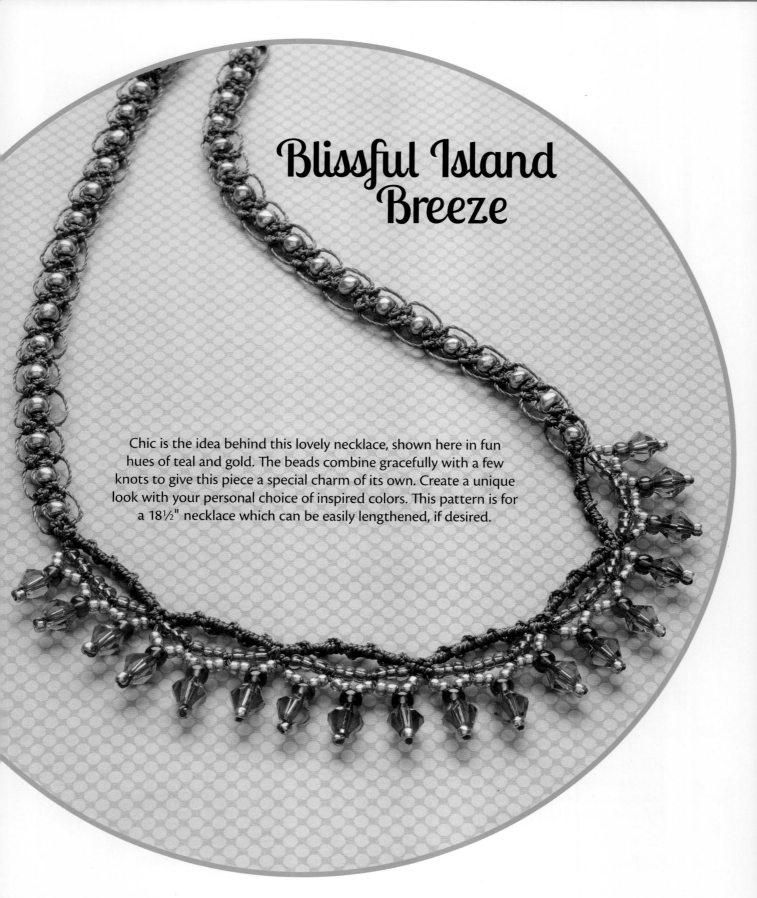

Blissful Island Breeze

Chic is the idea behind this lovely necklace, shown here in fun hues of teal and gold. The beads combine gracefully with a few knots to give this piece a special charm of its own. Create a unique look with your personal choice of inspired colors. This pattern is for a 18½" necklace which can be easily lengthened, if desired.

Supplies

- Cerulean C-Lon cord:
  3 cords, 10' each
- **36** 6º gold seed beads
- **18** 6º dark teal seed beads
- **90** 10º gold seed beads
- **54** 3mm aqua blue beads
- **18** 5mm bicone aqua blue beads
- **2** 6mm gold jump rings
- Gold lobster clasp
- **2** Pairs of chainnose pliers

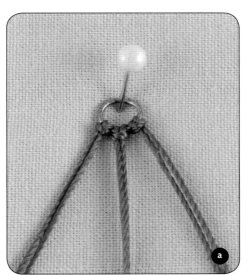

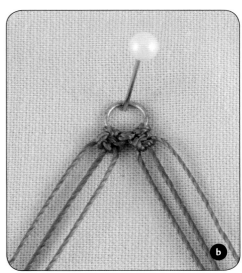

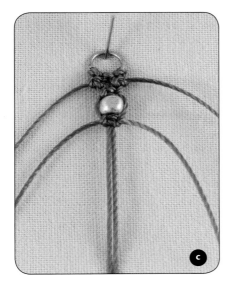

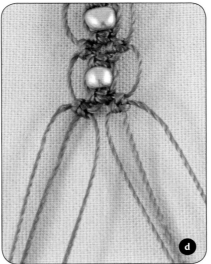

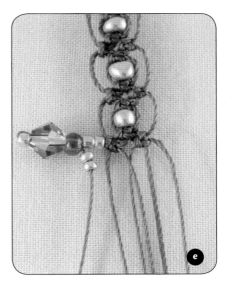

Instructions

1. Fold a cord in half and attach it to a jump ring using a lark's head knot (**Basics, p.10**). Repeat with the remaining two cords (**a**).

2. Separate cords 3-3. Tie a square knot (**Basics, p. 11**) with each set of cords (**b**).

3. Separate cords 1-4-1 and tie a square knot with the four center cords. Thread a 6º gold seed bead on the two center cords. Tie another square knot with the four center cords (**c**).

4. Repeat steps 2 and 3 until you have 18 6º gold beads, ending after step 2 (**d**).

5. Thread beads onto the left cord in the following order: two 10º gold seed beads, a 6º teal seed bead, a 5mm aqua bicone, a 10º gold seed bead. Thread the cord back through the 5mm bicone bead and the 6º teal bead. Thread two 10º gold beads onto the cord (**e**).

6. Take the second cord from the left and thread three 3mm aqua blue beads.

7. Use the left cord to tie a vertical lark's head knot (**Basics, p.16**) onto the second cord in from the left (**f**).

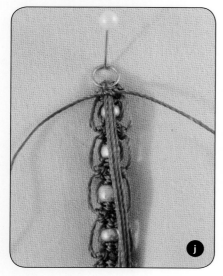

The center of this piece gives us a glimpse into the world of knotted lace, also known as Margaretenspitze (or Margarete Lace) originally designed by Margarete Naumann. Tying half-hitch knots around several cords creates a bundle technique that is common to Margarete Lace.

8. Repeat steps 5–7 twice **(g)**.

9. Using the right cord, tie double half-hitch knots around the three cords next to it for about 3/4". The double half-hitch knot is tied the same way as a diagonal double half-hitch knot, but instead of moving the holding cord to the diagonal, keep the holding cord vertical. (Each time you repeat this step, find the longest cord of the four right cords and move it to the right to use as the wrapping cord.) **(h)**.

10. Place all cords together. Use the left cord and the right cord to tie a square knot around all other cords **(i)**.

11. Repeat steps 5–10 five times.

12. Repeat steps 2–4.

13. Thread a jump ring onto the four center cords. Turn to the back side of the necklace. Now rotate the piece so the jump ring is at the top of your board. Bring the four center cords back toward you, laying them on top of the necklace. Use the outer cord on each side to tie a square knot around the center cords (but not around the necklace). Place a dab of glue on the last knot and let it dry. Trim the excess cords **(j)**.

14. Add a lobster clasp with one of the jump rings **(Basics, p. 17).**

On a Whim

Donut beads can sometimes be hard to find, especially in bright colors. So if you see one you like, buy it! You might want to use it in this pattern which features waxed cord. Interestingly, you can't use a soft cord like C-Lon for this design; only stiff cords that retain their shape will work. The finished length is about 20".

Supplies

- Turquoise waxed cord: 6 cords, 6' each
- 6º aqua seed bead
- 4 10º aqua seed beads
- **140** 10º lime green seed beads
- 1½" green & blue donut bead
- **2** silver jump rings
- Silver lobster claw clasp
- **2** Pairs chainnose pliers
- Glue

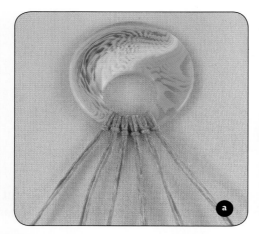

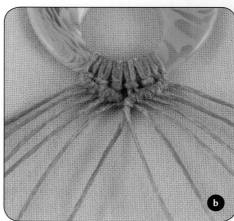

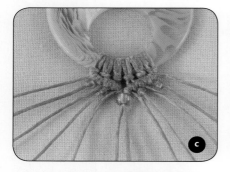

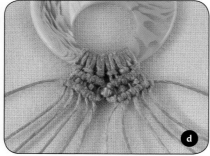

Instructions

1. Fold a cord in half to find the center, then attach it to the donut ring using a lark's head knot **(Basics, p. 10)**. Repeat with the remaining five cords **(a)**.

2. Separate cords 6-6. With the left six cords, move the left cord to the right as the holding cord. Tie a horizontal double half-hitch knot **(Basics, p. 15)** onto it with each of the five cords from left to right.

3. With the right six cords, move the right cord to the left as the holding cord. Tie a horizontal double half-hitch knot onto it with each of the five cords from right to left **(b)**.

4. Thread the two center cords through a 6º aqua seed bead. Now, thread a 10º aqua seed bead onto the second and fourth cord from the center outward on both sides **(c)**.

5. Move the left center cord over the right cords as the holding cord. Tie a horizontal double half-hitch knot with each of the right five cords onto the holding cord from the inside to the outside. Move the right center cord over the left cords as the holding cord. Tie a horizontal double half-hitch knot with each of the left five cords onto the holding cord from the inside to the outside **(d)**.

6. Separate cords 3-3-3-3. Tie a square knot **(Basics, p. 11)** with each set of three cords **(e)**.

7. Separate cords 6-6. Tie a square knot with the four center cords of each section **(f)**.

With the left six cords:

8. On the third cord from the right, thread a 10º lime green seed bead, then tie a vertical lark's head knot **(Basics, p. 16)** around the fourth cord in from the right **(g)**.

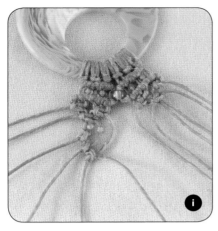

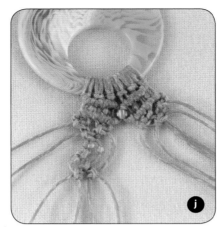

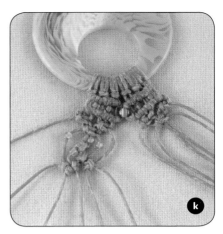

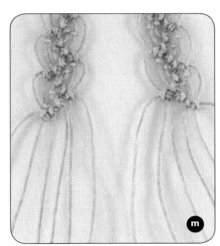

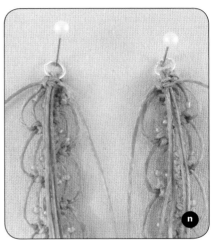

9. On the second cord from the right, thread a 10º lime green bead, then tie a vertical lark's head knot around the third cord from the right **(h)**.

10. Use the outer right cord to tie a vertical lark's head knot around the second cord from the right **(i)**.

11. On the third cord from the left, thread a 10º lime green bead, then tie a vertical lark's head knot onto the fourrth cord from the left **(j)**.

12. On the second cord from the left, thread a 10º lime green bead, then tie a vertical lark's head knot onto the third cord from the left **(k)**.

13. Use the outer left cord to tie a vertical lark's head knot onto the second cord from the left **(l)**.

14. Repeat steps 8–13 for a length of about 10".

With the right six cords:
15. On the third cord from the right, thread a 10º lime green bead, then tie a vertical lark's head knot around the fourth cord from the right.

16. On the second cord from the right, thread a 10º lime green bead, then tie a vertical lark's head knot around the third cord from the right.

17. Use the outer right cord to tie a vertical lark's head knot around the second cord from right.

18. On the third cord from the left, thread a 10º lime green bead, then tie a vertical lark's head knot onto the fourth cord from the left.

19. On the second cord from the left, thread a 10º lime green bead, then tie a vertical lark's head knot onto the third cord from the left.

20. Use the outer left cord to tie a vertical lark's head knot onto the second cord in from the left.

21. Repeat steps 15–20 for a length of about 10" **(m)**.

22. On one end, thread a jump ring onto the four center cords. Turn to the back side of the necklace. Rotate the necklace so the jump ring is at the top of your board. Bring the four center cords back toward you, laying them on top of the necklace. Use the outer cord on each side to tie a square knot around the center cords (but not around the necklace). Place a dab of glue on the last knot and let it dry. Trim the excess cords. Repeat on the opposite side of the necklace. Use chainnose pliers to open a jump ring **(Basics, p. 17)**. Add a lobster clasp with one of the jump rings and close the ring **(n)**.

Once Upon a Time

Begin with a large focal pendant, then choose coordinating beads to enhance it. I chose cream, gold, and peach beads to adorn apricot C-Lon cord and to create a backdrop for this embellished pendant. The finished knotted length is about 18".

Supplies

Necklace
- Apricot C-Lon cord:
  4 cords, 8' each
- **60** 11º cream seed beads
- **60** 11º peach seed beads
- **160** 11º gold seed beads
- **8** 6mm peach beads
- **4** 5mm gold jump rings
- Lobster claw clasp
- **2** pairs of chainnose pliers
- Glue

Pendant
- **3** 3mm freshwater pearls
- **2** 6º cream seed beads
- **8** 6º peach seed beads
- 6mm peach bead
- **4** gold head pins
- **2** gold eye pins
- 5mm gold jump ring
- 15mm gold ring
- **2** gold leaves
- Focal pendant

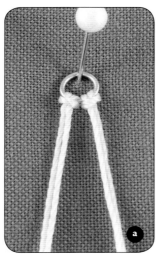

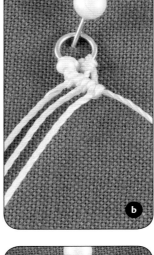

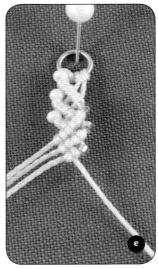

Instructions
Necklace

1. Fold a cord in half to find the center and attach it to a 5mm jump ring using a lark's head knot (**Basics, p. 10**). Repeat with a second cord **(a)**.

2. Thread an 11º cream seed bead onto the left cord, then move this cord to the right as the holding cord. Tie a diagonal double half-hitch knot (**Basics, p. 13**) onto the holding cord with each of the next three cords **(b)**.

3. Thread an 11º cream bead onto the left cord and move it to the right as the holding cord. Tie a diagonal double half-hitch knot onto the holding cord with each of the next two cords **(c)**.

4. Thread an 11º cream bead onto the left cord and move it to the right as the holding cord. Tie a diagonal double half-hitch knot onto the holding cord with the next cord **(d)**.

5. Thread an 11º gold seed bead onto the right cord and move it to the left as the holding cord. Tie a diagonal double half-hitch knot onto the holding cord with each of the next three cords.

6. Thread an 11º gold bead onto the right cord and move it to the left as the holding cord. Tie a diagonal double half-hitch knot onto the holding cord with each of the next two cords.

7. Thread an 11º gold bead onto the right cord and place it to the left as the holding cord. Tie a diagonal double half-hitch knot onto the holding cord with the next cord **(e)**.

8. Thread an 11º peach seed bead onto the left cord and move it to the right as the holding cord. Tie a diagonal double half-hitch knot onto

the holding cord with each of the next three cords.

9. Thread an 11º peach bead onto the left cord and move it to the right as the holding cord. Tie a diagonal double half-hitch knot onto the holding cord with each of the next two cords.

10. Thread an 11º peach bead onto the left cord and move it to the right as the holding cord. Tie a diagonal double half-hitch knot onto the holding cord with the next cord **(f)**.

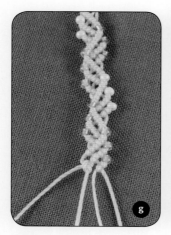

11. Thread an 11º cream bead onto the right cord and move it to the left as the holding cord. Tie a diagonal double half-hitch knot onto the holding cord with each of the next three cords. Thread an 11º cream bead onto the right cord and move it to the left as the holding cord. Tie a diagonal double half-hitch knot onto the holding cord with each of the next two cords. Thread an 11º cream bead onto the right cord and move it to the left as the holding cord. Tie a diagonal double half-hitch knot onto the holding cord with the next cord.

12. Thread an 11º gold bead onto the left cord and move it to the right as the holding cord. Tie a diagonal double half-hitch knot onto the holding cord with each of the next three cords. Thread an 11º gold bead onto the left cord and move it to the right as the holding cord. Tie a diagonal double half-hitch knot onto the holding cord with each of next two cords.

Thread an 11º gold bead onto the left cord and move it to the right as the holding cord. Tie a diagonal double half-hitch knot onto the holding cord with the next cord.

13. Thread an 11º peach bead onto the right cord and move it to the left as the holding cord. Tie a diagonal double half-hitch knot onto the holding cord with each of next three cords. Thread an 11º peach bead onto the right cord and move it to the left as the holding cord. Tie a diagonal double half-hitch knot onto the holding cord with each of the next two cords. Thread an 11º peach bead onto the right cord and move it to the left as the holding cord. Tie a diagonal double half-hitch knot onto the holding cord with the next cord.

14. Find the left cord and use it to tie a vertical lark's head knot (**Basics, p. 16**) onto the cord next to it (**g**).

15. Take the outer left cord and the outer right cord and tie a square knot (**Basics, p. 11**) around the two center cords.

16. Thread a 6mm peach bead onto the two center cords. Thread six 11º gold beads onto each outer cord. Use the outer cords to tie a square knot around the two center cords (**h**).

17. Repeat steps 2–16 three times.

18. Repeat steps 2–15.

19. Turn to the back side of the piece. Rotate the necklace so the loose cords are at the top of your board. Thread the two center cords through a jump ring and bring them down toward you, laying them on top of the necklace. Use the outer cord on each side to tie a square knot around the center cords (but not around the necklace). Place a dab of glue on the last knot and let it dry. Trim excess cords (**i**).

20. Repeat steps 1–19, attaching the new C-Lon cords to the same jump ring you started with.

21. Attach a lobster claw clasp to one of the jump rings (**Basics, p. 17**).

Pendant
22. Feel free to assemble the pendant anyway you desire. Here is what I did: I placed various beads on gold headpins, made plain loops (**Basics, p. 17**) and attached them to a 15mm gold ring. I used two gold eye pins to dangle leaves from the bottom of the ring and beaded above them. I then attached the pendant to the center of the necklace with another jump ring (**j**).

One Thousand Wishes

I was able to find just the right bead colors and shapes to work with my new navy C-Lon cord. I really enjoyed the way the centerpiece came together in this arrangement. It worked out to be a somewhat dainty piece, which can be enticing in a choker. This project measures about 12" with an adjustable closure.

Supplies

- Navy C-Lon cord:
  3 cords, 9' each
- **17** 6° black diamond seed bead mix
- 10° clear seed bead
- **57** 2mm iridescent cube beads (cube shape is optional)
- 5mm dark blue teardrop bead
- 6mm blue-black round bead
- Adjustable silver fold-over crimp end with adjustable clasp
- Chainnose pliers
- Glue

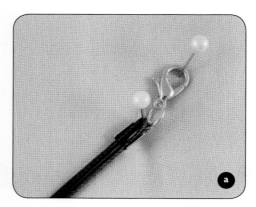

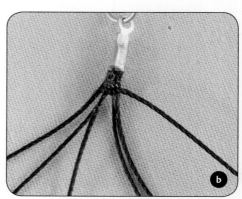

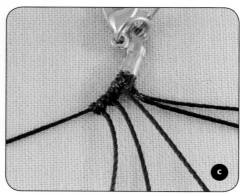

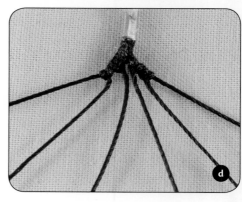

Instructions

1. Position all three cords together and fold them in half. Place a dab of glue on the fold-over crinmp end, then add cords as shown **(a)**. Using chainnose pliers, close the crimp end, then turn it over **(Basics, p. 17)**.

2. Using the third cord from the right, tie a diagonal double half-hitch knot **(Basics, p. 13)** onto the third cord from the left **(b)**.

3. Move the third cord from the left down and to the left as the holding cord. Tie a diagonal double half-hitch knot onto it with each of the remaining two left cords, from inside to outside **(c)**.

4. Move the third cord from the right down and to the right as the holding cord. Tie a diagonal double half-hitch knot onto it with each of the remaining two right cords, from inside to outside **(d)**.

5. Separate cords 1-4-1. Using the four center cords, place the two center cords together. Tie a square knot **(Basics, p. 11)** around them with the cord to the left and the cord to the right **(e)**.

6. Separate cords 3-3. Move the outer left cord down and to the right. Tie a diagonal double half-hitch knot onto it with the remaining two left cords, outside to inside. Move the outer right cord down and to the left. Tie a diagonal double half-hitch knot onto it with the remaining two right cords, outside to inside **(f)**.

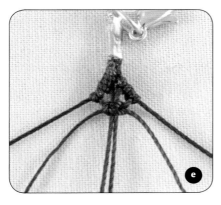

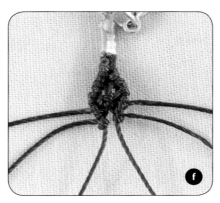

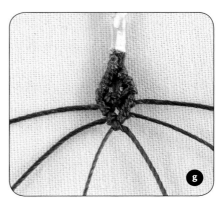

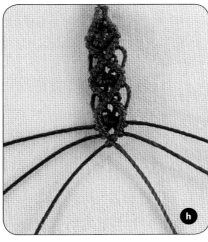

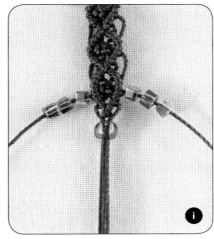

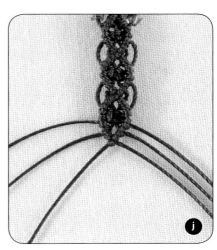

7. Using the two center cords, move the right cord to the left as the holding cord. Tie a diagonal double half-hitch knot onto it with the left cord to close the diamond shape **(g)**.

8. Repeat steps 3–7 twice, giving you three complete diamonds **(h)**.

9. Separate cords 1-4-1. Thread a 6º blue seed bead onto the four center cords and three 2mm iridescent cube beads onto the outer cord of each side **(i)**.

10. Repeat steps 2–8 **(j)**.

11. Repeat step 9.

12. Repeat steps 2–8.

13. Repeat step 9.

14. Repeat steps 2–8.

15. Repeat step 9.

Adjustable clasps like the one used in this project are also called ribbon clasps or ribbon end sets. They can be found with a clamp at the end which is used for wide ribbons.

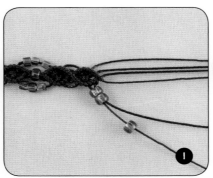

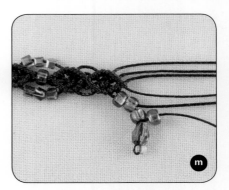

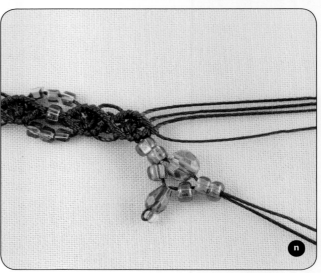

16. Repeat steps 2–7, then 3–7 just one time ending with two diamond shapes **(k)**.

For the center:

17. Turn the necklace so the worked section is horizontal and on the left. On the bottom two cords, thread two 6º blue beads. Thread a third 6º blue bead onto the lowest cord, only **(l)**.

18. On the lowest cord, thread a 5mm blue teardrop bead and a 10º clear bead. Thread this cord back through the teardrop bead from bottom to top. Thread a 6º blue bead onto this cord **(m)**.

19. Thread a 6mm blue bead onto the second cord from the bottom. Thread two more 6º beads onto both bottom cords. Rotate the necklace so it is vertical with the center beading on the left **(n)**.

20. With the right four cords: Thread three 2mm iridescent cube beads onto the right cord. Thread a 6º blue bead onto the remaining three cords.

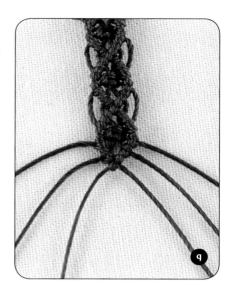

21. Tie two vertical lark's head knots **(Basics, p. 16)** with the right cord around the three cords with the 6º black bead **(o)**.

22. Repeat steps 10–21 once; then repeat step 20. End of center **(p)**.

23. Repeat steps 2–7, then 3–7 one time giving you two diamond shapes.

24. Repeat step 9.

25. Repeat steps 2–8 **(q)**.

26. Repeat step 9.

27. Repeat steps 2–8.

28. Repeat step 9.

29. Repeat steps 2–8.

30. Repeat step 9.

31. Repeat steps 2–8.

32. Turn the piece so the backside of the necklace is facing up. Place a dab of glue in the fold-over crimp end and lay the cords on top. Use chainnose pliers to close the crimp end. Trim the excess cords **(r)**.

Earrings & More

Silver Moon Glow

Celebrating silver, this design was created to complement the
Moonlit Waters bracelet found on page 28. These subtle, yet
sophisticated earrings enhance the bracelet without stealing the show.
Fnished length is about 1³⁄₁₆" of knotted work.

Supplies
- Silver C-Lon cord:
  4 cords, 18" each
- **2** 6º chrome seed beads
- **2** 10º silver seed beads
- **40** 11º gray seed beads
- **2** 6mm smoky gray beads
- **2** 4mm silver jump rings
- **2** Silver earring wires
- **2** Pairs of chainnose pliers
- Glue

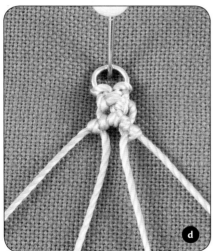

Instructions

1. Fold a cord a in half to find the center. Attach it to a silver jump ring using a lark's head knot **(Basics, p. 10)**. Repeat with a second cord **(a)**.

2. Tie a square knot **(Basics, p. 11)** with the left and right cords around the center two cords **(b)**.

3. Move the second cord from the right to the left as the holding cord. Tie a diagonal double half-hitch knot **(Basics, p. 13)** onto it with each of the two left cords, working from inside to outside **(c)**.

4. Move the second cord from the right to the right as the holding cord, over the top of the right cord. Tie a diagonal double half-hitch knot onto the holding cord with the right cord **(d)**.

5. Thread a 6º chrome seed bead onto the two center cords.

6. Thread three 11º gray seed beads onto the left cord. Move it to the right and tie a diagonal double half-hitch knot onto it with the second cord from the left **(e)**.

7. Thread three 11º gray beads onto the right cord. Move it to the left and tie a diagonal double half-hitch knot onto it with the second cord from the right **(f)**.

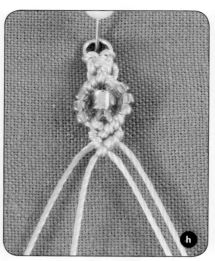

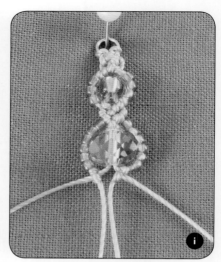

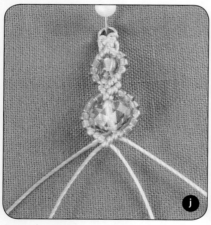

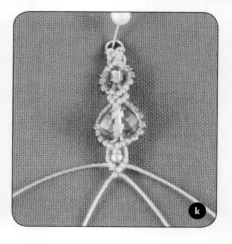

8. Move the right center cord over the left center cord. Tie a diagonal double half-hitch knot with the center left cord onto the center right cord (g).

9. Move the left cord to the right and tie a diagonal double half-hitch knot onto it with the second cord from the left. Move the right cord to the left and tie a diagonal double half-hitch knot onto it with the second and third cords from the right (h).

10. Thread both center cords through a 6mm smoky gray bead. Thread seven 11º gray beads onto each outer cord.

11. Move the left cord to the right and tie a diagonal double half-hitch knot onto it with the second cord from the left.

12. Move the right cord to the left and tie a diagonal double half-hitch knot onto it with the second cord from the right (i).

13. Move the right center cord over the left center cord. Tie a diagonal double half-hitch knot with the center left cord onto the center right cord (j).

14. Thread a 10º silver seed bead onto the two center cords. Move the left cord to the right. Tie a diagonal double half-hitch knot onto it with the second cord from the left. Move the right cord to the left and tie a diagonal double half-hitch knot onto it with the second cord from the right.

15. Move the right center cord over the left center cord. Tie a diagonal double half-hitch knot with the left cord onto the right (k).

16. Glue the back side of the final knot and allow to dry. Trim the excess cords.

17. Open an earring wire (**Basics, p. 17**) and attach it to the jump ring. Close the earring wire.

18. Repeat steps 1–17 for the second earring.

Morning Starlight

I had an idea about layering and decided to try my hand at it with this pattern. A metal accent piece backs up the knotted work, while a light chain offers another texture to the design. Finished length is about 2".

Supplies
- Steel C-Lon cord:
  8 cords, 24" each
- **2** 6º silver seed beads
- **28** 11º silver seed beads
- **2** 1" silver diamond-shaped accent piece
- **2** silver earring wires
- **6** 4mm silver jump rings
- **2** 6mm silver jump rings
- 9" small, silver chain
- Wire cutters
- **2** Pairs of chainnose pliers
- Glue

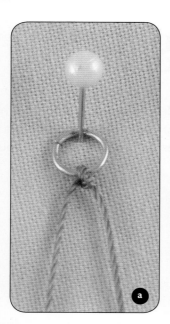

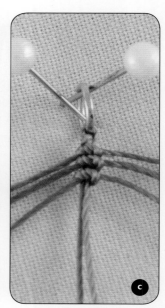

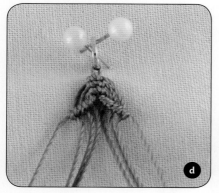

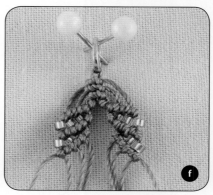

Instructions

1. Thread a 6mm silver jump ring onto a 24" cord and move it to the center. (Keep the opening of jump ring accessible.) Tie an overhand knot (**Basics, p. 10**) **(a)**.

2. Center a 24" cord horizontally under the two cords on the jump ring. Tie it onto both cords with an overhand knot. Repeat with two more cords **(b)**.

3. Turn the jump ring on it's side and pin it in place as shown. Tug the cords gently until they are flat against your board **(c)**.

4. Separate cords 4-4. Right four cords: Move the left cord down and to the right as the holding cord, then tie a diagonal double half-hitch knot (**Basics, p. 13**) onto it with each remaining cord from inside to outside.

5. Left four cords: Move the right cord down and to the left as the holding cord, then tie a diagonal double half-hitch knot onto it with each remaining cord from inside to outside **(d)**.

6. Still working with the four left cords: Thread an 11º silver seed bead onto the first, second, and third cords from the left. Move the fourth cord

from the left, down and out to the left as the holding cord. Tie a diagonal double half-hitch knot onto it with each of the other three left cords from inside to outside.

7. Right four cords: Thread an 11º silver seed bead onto the first, second, and third cords from the right. Move the fourth cord from the right, down and out to the right as the holding cord. Tie a diagonal double half-hitch knot onto it with each of the other three right cords from inside to outside **(e)**.

8. Left four cords: Thread an 11º silver bead onto the first and second cords from the

left. Move the fourth cord from the left, down and out to the left as the holding cord. Tie a diagonal double half-hitch knot onto it with each of the other three left cords from inside to outside.

9. Right four cords: Thread an 11º silver bead onto the first and second cords from the right. Move the fourth cord from the right, down and out to the right as the holding cord. Tie a diagonal double half-hitch knot onto it with each of the other three right cords from inside to outside **(f)**.

10. Repeat steps 8 and 9 **(g)**.

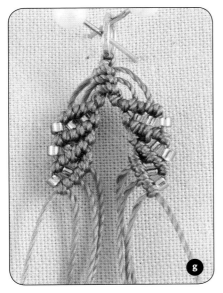

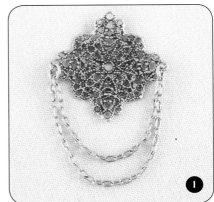

11. Place the two center cords together. Using the third cord from the right, tie a vertical lark's head knot (**Basics, p. 16**) around both center cords. Add this tying cord to the holding cords. Tie a vertical lark's head knot around these holding cords with the third cord from the left (**h**).

12. Thread the four center cords through a 6° silver seed bead (**i**).

13. Separate cords 4-4. Move the outer right cord down and left as the holding cord. Tie a diagonal double half-hitch knot onto it with each of the three right cords, from outside to inside.

14. Move the outer left cord down and right as the holding cord. Tie a diagonal double half-hitch knot onto it with each of the left three cords, from outside to inside.

15. Find the two center cords and place the right cord over the top of the left. Tie a diagonal double half-hitch knot with the left cord onto the right cord (**j**).

16. Place a dab of glue on the back of each diagonal double half-hitch knot and let the glue dry. Carefully trim off each cord.

17. Using wire cutters, cut a 2" length of silver chain. Use chainnose pliers to attach each end to a 4mm silver jump ring (**Basics, p. 17**).

18. Cut a 2½" length of silver chain and attach each end to the same jump rings as the shorter lengths of chain (**k**).

19. Attach chained jump rings to the accent piece (**l**).

20. Thread the accent piece onto the 6mm jump ring behind the knotted piece. Attach a 4mm jump ring to the 6mm jump ring. Attach a silver earring wire to the 4mm jump ring (**m**).

21. Repeat steps 1–20 for the second earring.

Constant Hope

I have always liked polished stones, so I really enjoyed finding the purple agates used here. Working with waxed linen, these earrings come together with several fun knots including the diagonal double half-hitch knot, the square knot, and the vertical lark's head knot. The finished length is about 1³⁄₁₆" of knotted work.

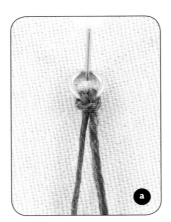

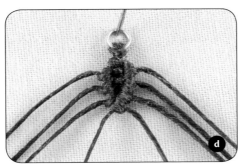

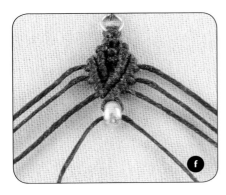
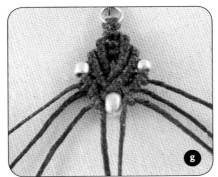
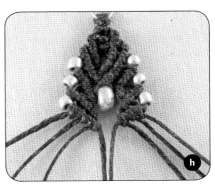

Supplies
- 1-ply, plum Irish waxed cord:
    8 cords, 22"
- **2** 6º silver seed beads
- **24** 10º silver seed beads
- **2** 6mm purple agate beads
- **2** silver earring wires
- **2** 4mm (or larger) silver jump rings
- **2** Pairs of chainnose pliers
- Glue

Instructions

1. Fold a cord in half to find the center, then attach it to a silver jump ring using a lark's head knot (**Basics, p. 10**) **(a)**.

tip: I find it's often easier to thread the cut ends of the cord through small spaces, instead of the folded center.

2. Center another cord horizontally under both cords and tie an overhand knot (**Basics, p. 10**). Repeat with two more cords **(b)**.

3. Separate the cords 4-4. Move the top left cord down and right as the holding cord. Tie a diagonal double half-hitch knot (**Basics, p. 13**) onto it with each of the three left cords, working from outside to inside.

4. Move the top right cord down and left as the holding cord. Tie a diagonal double half-hitch knot onto it with each of the three right cords, working from outside to inside **(c)**.

5. Using the center two cords, move the right cord over the left and tie a diagonal double half-hitch knot with the left cord onto the right cord **(d)**.

6. Repeat steps 3–5 **(e)**.

7. Using the center two cords, thread the left cord onto a 6º silver seed bead from the left. Then thread the right cord in from the right **(f)**.

8. Thread a 10º silver seed bead onto the top left cord. Move this cord down and in to the right as the holding cord. Tie a diagonal double

half-hitch knot onto this cord with each of the next three cords working from outside to inside.

9. Thread a 10º silver bead onto the top right cord. Move this cord down and to the left as the holding cord. Tie a diagonal double half-hitch knot onto this cord with each of the next three cords working from outside to inside **(g)**.

10. Repeat steps 8 and 9 twice **(h)**.

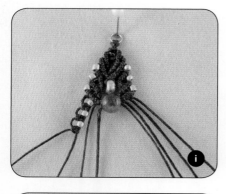
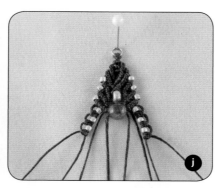
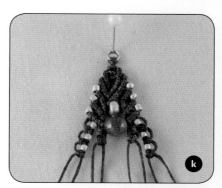

11. On the center two cords, thread a 6mm purple bead, threading one cord in from each side.

12. On the second cord from the left, thread a 10º silver bead. Using the left cord, tie a vertical lark's head knot **(Basics, p. 16)** onto the beaded cord, leaving a slight loop on the outer cord. Repeat twice **(i)**.

13. On the second cord from the right, thread a 10º silver bead. Using the right cord, tie a vertical lark's head knot onto the beaded cord, leaving a slight loop on the outer cord. Repeat twice **(j)**.

14. Use the third cord from the left to tie two vertical lark's head knots onto the fourth cord from the left.

15. Use the third cord from the right to tie two vertical lark's head knots onto the fourth cord from the right **(k)**.

16. Move the third cord from the left to the right as the holding cord. Tie a diagonal double half-hitch knot onto it with the fourth cord from the left.

17. Move the third cord from the right to the left as the holding cord. Tie a diagonal double half-hitch knot onto it with the fourth cord from the right **(l)**.

18. Using the center two cords, move the right cord over the left and tie a diagonal double half-hitch knot with the left cord onto the right cord.

19. Separate the cords 4-4. Use the left cord and tie a vertical lark's head knot around the three cords next to it.

20. Use the right cord to tie a vertical lark's head knot around the three cords next to it **(m)**.

21. Using the four center cords, place the two middle cords together, then use the left and right cord to tie a square knot **(Basics, p. 11) (n)**.

22. Place a dab of glue on the backside of the square knot and allow to dry. Carefully trim off each cord.

23. Open the loop of an earring wire **(Basics, p. 17)** and attach it to the jump ring.

24. Repeat steps 1–23 to make a second earring.

Autumn Daydreams

Worked from the bottom to the top, half-knots and diagonal double half-hitch knots combine to create these graceful earrings. Copper rose C-Lon cord complements the copper beads and metal connector. The finished length is about 2¼" (measured from the connector bead to the bottom of the dangling bead).

Supplies

- Copper rose C-Lon cord:
     10 cords, 24" each
- **44** 10º copper seed beads
- **2** 15mm copper filigree connectors
- **2** 6mm copper jump rings
- **4** 6mm copper rose beads
- **2** Copper head pins
- **2** Copper earring wire
- **2** Pair chainnose pliers
- Glue

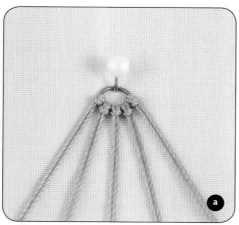

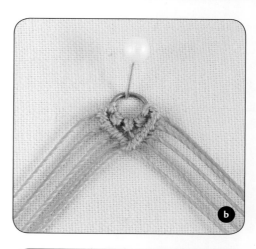

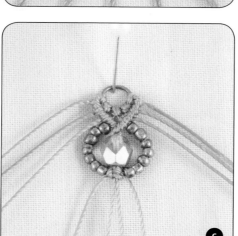

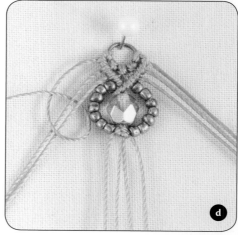

Instructions

1. Fold a cord in half to find the center. Attach it to a 6mm jump ring using a lark's head knot **(Basics, p. 10)**. Repeat with four more cords **(a)**.

2. Separate cords 5-5. Move the outer left cord to the right as the holding cord. Tie a diagonal double half-hitch knot **(Basics, p. 13)** with each remaining cord from the outside to the inside. Move the outer right cord to the left as the holding cord. Tie a double half-hitch knot with each remaining cord from the outside to the inside. Move the right center cord over the left center cord. Tie a diagonal double half-hitch knot with left cord onto the right **(b).**

3. Thread the two center cords through a 6mm copper rose bead. Thread seven 10º copper seed beads onto the fourth cord from the left and onto the fourth cord from the right. Tie a square knot **(Basics, p. 11)** with the beaded cords around the two center cords **(c)**.

4. With the three left cords, use the outer cord to tie double half-hitch knots around the other two. The double half-hitch knot is tied the same as a diagonal double half-hitch knot, but instead of moving the holding cord to the diagonal, keep the holding cord vertical. Repeat for the length of about ⅝" **(d)**.

5. With the three right cords, use the outer cord to tie a double half-hitch knot around the other two. (As in step 4, the double half-hitch knot is tied the same as a diagonal double half-hitch knot, but instead of moving the holding cord to the diagonal, keep the holding cord vertical.) Repeat for the length of about ⅝" **(e)**.

6. Left three cords: thread a 10º copper bead onto the outer cord. Move it to the right as the holding cord. Tie a diagonal double half-hitch knot onto it with each of the remaining two cords. Repeat twice.

7. Right three cords: Thread a 10º copper bead onto the outer cord. Move it to the left as the holding cord. Tie a diagonal double half-hitch knot onto it with each of the remaining two cords. Repeat twice **(f)**.

8. Center four cords: Move the second cord from the right to the left as the holding cord. Tie a diagonal double half-hitch knot onto it with each of the next two cords. Move the second cord from the right to the right, and tie a diagonal double half-hitch knot onto it with the right cord. The center two cords are now crossed and we will leave them that way. Move the left cord to the right and tie a diagonal double half-hitch knot onto it with

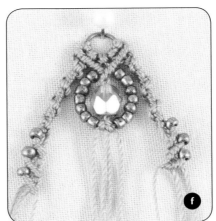

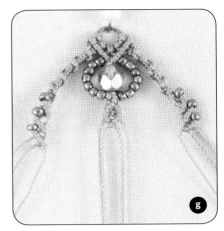

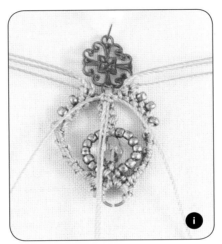

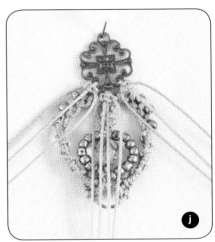

the next cord. Move the right cord to the left and tie a diagonal double half-hitch knot onto it with the next cord. Close by tying a diagonal double half-hitch knot with the center left cord onto the center right cord (g).

9. Separate the cords 5-5. Move the inner left cord to the left as the holding cord, then tie a diagonal double half-hitch knot onto it with each remaining cord from inside to outside. Move the inner right cord to the right as the holding cord, then tie a diagonal double half-hitch knot onto it with each remaining cord from inside to outside. (h).

10. Turn the piece over to the back, then rotate it so the jump ring is at the bottom of your work surface. Separate cords 3-4-3. Place the copper connector piece with the back side facing up near the four center cords. Working with the four center cords, move the middle two cords through the lowest opening of the connector piece from the front to the back. Bring these two cords back over the knots. Use the two side cords to tie a square knot (i).

11. Using the left three cords, thread the center cord through the connector piece from front to back. Bring the cord back over the knots and tie a square knot with the

other two cords. Repeat with the right three cords. Glue the square knots and trim the excess cords (j).

12. On a copper head pin, thread a 10° copper bead, a 6mm copper bead, and a 10° copper bead. Make a plain loop (Basics, p. 17), then attach it to the copper jump ring (Basics, p. 17). Attach a copper earring wire to the top of the connector piece (k).

13. Repeat steps 1–12 to make a second earring.

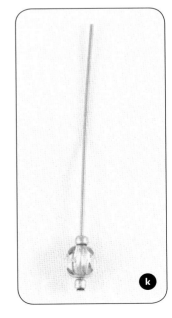

Arabian Nights anklet

Here we take the idea from the Button Clasp Bracelet and expand upon it by adding a row of draping, dangling beads. The unique centerpiece further changes this design from the original bracelet. Choose a center bead with a large diameter hole as this pattern places five cords through it, then embellish it with a complementary charm. The finished length is about 9".

Supplies
- White C-Lon cord:
  - **1** 7' cord
  - **2** 6' cords
- **14** 6° medium blue seed beads
- **78** 10° medium blue seed beads
- **90** 10° silver seed beads
- **12** 5mm light blue round beads
- 13mm light blue center bead
- 15mm silver charm with jump ring
- Silver jump ring
- 10mm silver ring
- Silver lobster claw clasp
- Glue

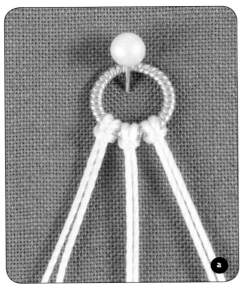

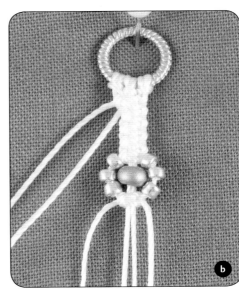

Instructions

1. Fold one of the 6' cords in half and attach it to the 10mm silver ring using a lark's head knot (**Basics, p. 10**). Repeat with second 6' cord.

2. On the 7' cord, measure from one end up 1'. Fold here so you have 1' on one side of the cord and 6' on the other. Hold it so the short cord is on the right and place the fold through the silver ring—to the left of all other cords—from front to back. Attach using a lark's head knot. As long as your cord did not twist, you will end up with the short cord being the second cord from the left (**a**).

3. Use the left cord and the right cord to tie a square knot (**Basics, p. 11**) around the remaining a cords. Separate the cords 2-4.

4. Using the right four cords, use the left and right cord to tie four square knots. Thread a 6° blue seed bead onto the center two cords. Thread three 10° silver seed beads onto each outer cord. Move all four cords together and tie a square knot (**b**).

5. Repeat the previous step six times, then tie three square knots.

6. Working with the left two cords only, use the left cord to tie seven vertical lark's head knots (**Basics, p. 16**) around the right cord (**c**).

7. Thread three 10° medium blue seed beads onto the left cord followed by a 3mm light blue bead and three more 10° medium blue beads. Tie a vertical lark's head knot with the left cord onto the right, then slide it up tight against the previous knots. Tie six more vertical lark's head knots.

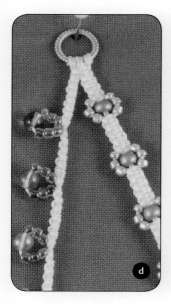

8. Repeat step 7 five times. **(d)**.

9. Move all cords together. Use the left cord to tie a vertical lark's head knot around all the other cords. Thread the left cord as follows: three 10° silver beads, three 10° blue beads, silver charm, three 10° blue beads, three 10° silver beads. Thread the right five cords through the 13mm blue bead. Tie a vertical lark's head knot with the left cord around all others **(e)**.

10. Separate cords 2-4, making sure the shortest cord is the second cord in from the left. Working with the left two cords, use the outer cord to tie seven vertical lark's head knots around the right cord.

11. Repeat steps 7 and 8.

12. Using the right four cords, move the shortest two cords into the center. Use the left and right cord to tie three square knots.

13. Thread a 6° blue bead onto the center two cords. Thread three 10° silver seed beads onto each outer cord. Place all four cords together and tie a square knot. Tie four more square knots. Repeat six times **(f)**.

14. Position all cords together and tie a square knot with the left and right cord.

15. Add a jump ring to the lobster claw clasp if necessary **(Basics, p. 17)**. Turn to the back side of the anklet. Rotate the piece so the loose cords are at the top of your board. Thread the jump ring onto the center four cords, then bring them back toward you, laying them on top of the anklet. Use the outer cord on each side to tie a square knot around the center cords (but not around the anklet). Place a dab of glue on the last knot and let it dry. Trim the excess cords **(g)**.

Black Cherry Ice watchband

I love this beautiful watch face. It comes to life with this striking watchband enhanced with silver crystals. Find an old watch face at an antique store or purchase a new one in a style you like, then add this band in complementary colors. The finished length is about 6½" and has an adjustable clasp.

Supplies:
- Red C-Lon cord:
  8 cords, 3' each
- **20** 2mm charcoal beads
- **4** 6mm dark silver bicones
- **2** 8mm dark red bicones
- 1⅜" x 1⁷⁄₁₆" watch face
- **4** Silver jump rings
- Silver adjustable lobster claw clasp
- Fold-over crimp end with extender chain
- **2** Pairs of chainnose pliers
- Glue

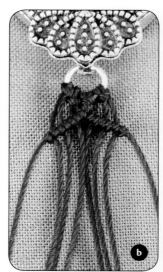

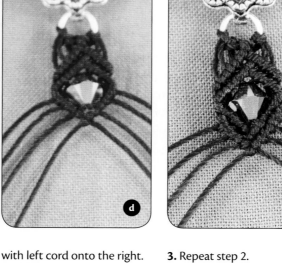

Instructions:

1. Attach a jump ring onto one side of the watchband **(Basics, p. 17)**. Fold a red C-Lon cord in half and find the center. Attach it to the jump ring using a lark's head knot **(Basics, p. 10)**. Repeat with three more cords **(a)**.

2. Using the two center cords, move the right cord over the left. Tie a diagonal double half-hitch knot **(Basics, p. 13)** with left cord onto the right. Move the fourth cord from the left and move it to the left as the holding cord. Tie a diagonal double half-hitch knot onto it with each of the three left cords, from inside to outside. Find the fourth cord from the right and move it to the right as the holding cord. Tie a diagonal double half-hitch knot onto it with each of the three right cords, from inside to outside **(b)**.

3. Repeat step 2.

4. On the two center cords, thread a 6mm dark silver bicone **(c)**.

5. Move the outer left cord to the right as the holding cord. Tie a diagonal double half-hitch knot onto it with the next three cords, from outside to inside.

6. Move the outer right cord to the left as the holding cord. Tie a diagonal double half-hitch knot onto it with the next three cords, from outside to inside.

7. Move the right center cord over the left center cord and tie a diagonal double half-hitch knot with the left cord **(d)**.

8. Repeat steps 5–7 **(e)**.

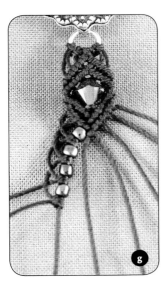

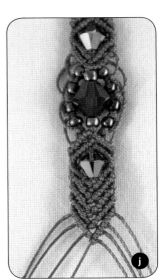

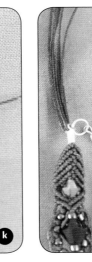

9. On the third cord in from the left, thread a 2mm charcoal bead. Use the outer left cord to tie a vertical lark's head knot (**Basics, p. 16**) onto the third cord (**f**).

10. Thread a 2mm charcoal bead onto the third cord from the left. Use the new outer left cord to tie a vertical lark's head knot onto the third cord.

11. Repeat steps 9 and 10 (**g**).

12. On the third cord from the right, thread a 2mm charcoal bead. Use the outer right cord to tie a vertical lark's head knot onto the third cord.

13. Thread a 2mm charcoal bead onto the third cord from the right. Use the new outer right cord to tie a vertical lark's head knot onto the third cord.

14. Repeat steps 12 and 13.

15. On the two center cords, thread a 2mm charcoal bead, an 8mm dark red bicone bead, and a 2mm charcoal bead (**h**).

16. Repeat steps 2–8 (**i**).

17. Repeat step 8 three times (**j**).

18. Attach a jump ring to a lobster clasp, then thread the jump ring onto the six center cords. Turn to the back side of the bracelet. Rotate the piece so the jump ring is at the top of your board. Bring the six center cords back toward you, laying them on top of the bracelet. Use the outer cord on each side to tie a square knot (**Basics, p. 11**) around the center cords (but not around the watchband). Place a dab of glue on the square knot and let it dry. Trim the excess cords (**k**).

19. Repeat steps 1–18 to make the other side.

20. Finish by placing a dab of glue into the fold-over crimp end and lay all cords across it. Close the cord end with chainnose pliers and trim any excess (**Basics, p. 17**). Attach the extender chain (**l**).

Priceless Pearls hair chain

From barrettes to combs to hair chains, hair accessories make a statement. A soft, unique look is created here using bobby pins, pearls, and C-Lon cord. This design is something you won't find anywhere else in the micro-macramé world. The finished length is about 7".

Supplies

- Seashell C-Lon cord:
    3 cords 6' each
    1 cord 8'
- **52** 11º peach seed beads
- **8** 2mm bronzebeads
- **25** 3mm peach beads
- **2** 6mm peach pearl beads
- 10mm peach pearl beads
- **2** Bronze 3-to-1 connnectors
- **2** Bobby pins
- Glue

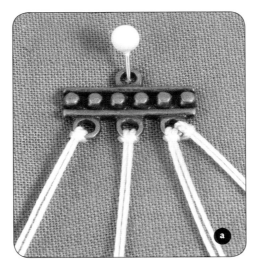

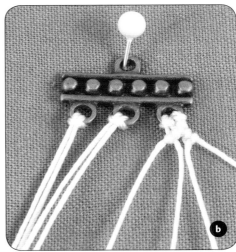

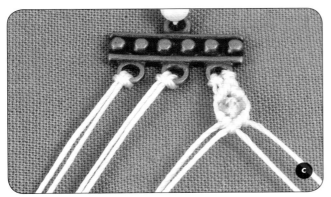

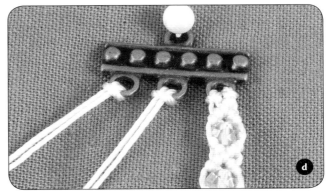

Instructions

1. On the 8' cord, measure up 3' from one end. Fold the cord here so that the 3' section is on the right. Attach this cord to the left loop on the 3-to-1 connector using a lark's head knot (**Basics, p. 10**). (As long as your cords don't twist, the short cord will end up on the right.)

2. Fold a 3' cord in half and attach it to the center loop using a lark's head knot Use a lark's head knot to attach the last two cords to the right loop of the connector (**a**).

3. Right four-cord section: Move the second cord from the right to the left as the holding cord. Tie a diagonal double half-hitch knot (**Basics, p. 13**) onto it with each of the two left cords, working from inside to outside. Move the second cord from the right to the right as the holding cord. Tie a diagonal double half-hitch knot onto it with the right cord (**b**).

4. Place a 3mm peach bead onto the center two cords. Move the left cord to the right and tie a diagonal double half-hitch knot onto it with the second cord from the left. Move the right cord to the left and tie a diagonal double half-hitch knot onto it with the second cord from the right. Using the center two cords, tie a diagonal double half-hitch knot onto the right cord with the left to close the diamond (**c**).

5. Move the second cord from the left to the left as the holding cord. Tie a diagonal double half-hitch knot onto it with the left cord. Move the second cord from the right to the right as the holding cord. Tie a diagonal double half-hitch knot onto it with the right cord. Place a 3mm peach bead onto the center two cords.

6. Move the left cord to the right and tie a diagonal double half-hitch knot onto it with the second cord from the left. Move the right cord to the left and tie a diagonal double half-hitch knot onto it with the second cord from the right. Using the center two cords, tie a diagonal diagonal double half-hitch knot onto the right cord with the left to close diamond (**d**).

7. Repeat steps 5 and 6. End of right cord section.

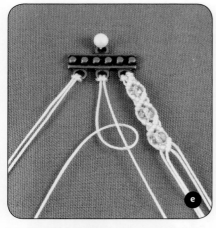

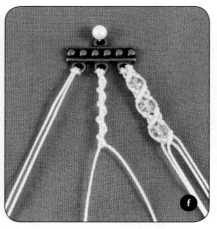

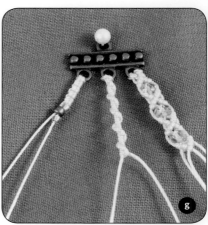

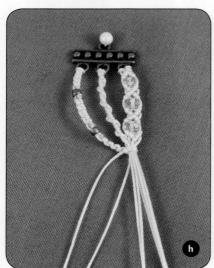

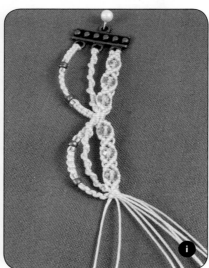

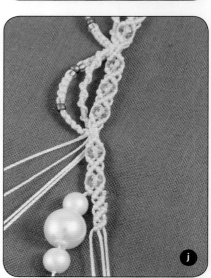

8. Using the center two cords, use the left cord to tie double half-hitch knots onto the remaining cord for about 1". The double half-hitch knot is tied the same as a diagonal double half-hitch knot, but instead of moving the holding cord to the diagonal, keep the holding cord vertical **(e, f)**.

9. Left two-cord section: Using the outer cord, tie four vertical lark's head knots onto the inner cord. Thread an 11º peach seed bead onto the right cord. Thread both cords through a 2mm bronze bead, then thread an 11º peach bead onto the right cord **(g)**.

10. Repeat step 9, then tie four vertical lark's head knots. End of left cord section.

11. Place all cords together and use the left cord to tie a vertical lark's head knot around all other cords **(h)**.

12. Repeat steps 3–11 **(i)**.

13. Repeat steps 3–6 with the right four cords.

14. Still working with the right four cords, thread a 6mm peach pearl bead onto the left cord followed by the 10mm pearl bead, then another 6mm pearl bead.

15. Thread an 11º peach bead onto the right cord and place it to the left as the holding cord. Tie a diagonal double half-hitch knot onto it with next two cords, working from outside to inside. Repeat twice **(j)**.

16. Use the second cord from the right to tie a vertical lark's head knot onto the third cord from the right. Thread three 11º peach beads onto the right cord then use it to tie a vertical lark's head knot around the second and third cords from the right **(k)**.

17. Thread a 11º peach bead onto the right cord. Move the left cord to the right as the

holding cord, then tie a diagonal double half-hitch knot with each of the next two cords from inside to outside. Repeat twice **(l)**.

18. Repeat steps 3–6 with the right four cords. End of right cord section.

19. Using the left two cords, use the outer cord to tie two vertical lark's head knots onto the inner cord. Thread a 3mm peach bead onto the inner cord and three 11º peach beads onto the outer cord. Tie two vertical lark's head knots with outer cord onto the inner cord **(m)**. Repeat twice.

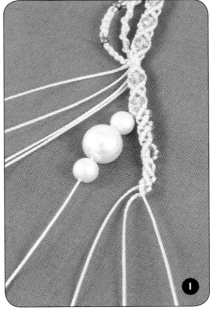

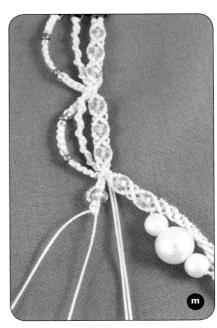

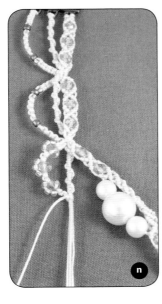

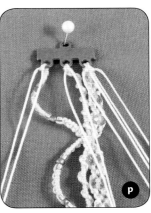

20. Set aside the two left cords. Using the center two cords, use the left cord to tie double half-hitch knots onto the remaining cord for a length of about ⅝". (As in step 8, the double half-hitch knot is tied the same as a diagonal double half-hitch knot, but instead of moving the holding cord to the diagonal, keep the holding cord vertical.)

21. Place the left four cords together and tie a vertical lark's head knot with the left cord around the other three **(n).**

22. Repeat steps 19–21 two times.

23. Place all cords together and use the left cord to tie a vertical lark's head knot around all cords **(o).**

24. Repeat steps 3–12.

25. Turn to the back of the piece and rotate it so the loose cords are at the top of the board. Place the 3-to-1 connector with the wrong side up near the loose cords.

26. Using the right four cords, thread the center two through the right opening on the clasp from front to back. Bring the two center cords back toward you, laying them over the knotted section. Use the left and right cords to

tie a square knot around the center two cords.

27. Set this section aside and find the center two cords. Thread the right cord through the center opening from front to back, and tie a diagonal double half-hitch knot with the left cord onto the right. Repeat with the last two cords, placing them through the left opening **(p).**

28. Glue the last knot of each section, then trim the excess cords. Place a bobby pin through the loop on each connector.

Woodland bracelet

Wild Cinnaman Fern bracelet

Island Cove necklace

Royalty necklace

Meandering Brook bracelet

Moon Dance pendant

Ackowledgments

I am just a girl who decided to go for it … thanks to my husband, without whom none of my books would have been written. He urged me to start somewhere and write a design or two, then he turned those few ideas into a self-published book, which in turn led to the opportunity to work with Kalmbach Publishing Company.

To all those who may need a gentle nudge … just go for it!

No matter how slow you go, you are still lapping everybody on the couch.
~ Anonymous

About the Author

As years of homeschooling her children began to come to an end, Kelsy realized she would soon be roaming her house with a cup of coffee in one hand, and too much time in the other. Looking for creative ways to fill her days and perhaps work from home, she soon discovered the little known genre of micro-macramé, which appealed to her in part because of its nominal startup costs. With encouragement from her husband, she lost no time in studying this art form, but soon realized that most of the projects available were written in the tightly woven *Cavandoli* technique. Yet the more open-weave style arrangements she favored, like *Margaretenspitze* (or Margarete Lace) were almost exclusively written in foreign languages. Always one to make a way where there is none, she purchased and waded through a book written in Italian. Soon after, Kelsy began developing her own patterns, adding her unique vision to the world of micro-macramé, She now has several books in print and has created over 40 original designs.

An Oregon native, Kelsy currently resides in the Ft. Worth area of Texas with her husband and youngest daughter, while their oldest daughter lives and works full time in Oregon. When not fashioning new works of art, she can be found reading or learning to stretch her creative boundaries with new activities, such as constructing antique miniature books and scrolls.

You can keep in touch with Kelsy at:
www.demure-designs.com and www.facebook.com/DemureDesigns

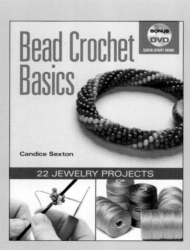

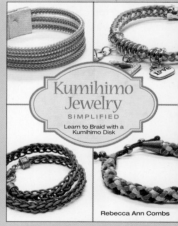